JUL 2 5 1989

D. R. MUZYKA

16 Ways to Avoid Saying No

16 Ways to Avoid Saying No

An Invitation to Experience Japanese
Management from the Inside

Masaaki Imai

THE NIHON KEIZAI SHIMBUN
(Japan Economic Journal)

THE NIHON KEIZAI SHIMBUN, INC.

1-9-5 Otemachi, Chiyoda-ku, Tokyo 100, Japan

Printed in Japan by The Dai Nippon Printing Co., Ltd.
ISBN4—532—08355—9

Author's Foreword

In the summer of 1977, at the 19th hole of the Chikuma Kogen Country Club, *Japan Economic Journal* editor Susumu Ohara suggested that I write an article a month about doing business in Japan for a special page entitled "News from Hotel Okura."

Since my office is only a stone's throw from the Hotel Okura, and since we have long respected the Okura as Japan's best, I was only too pleased at the opportunity to write for this fine hotel.

Writing regularly for the Okura and the *Journal* has been even more pleasurable than I had expected. Encouraging comments have been received from readers all over the world, and consequently I have made many new friends.

This book brings together articles carried in the *Japan Economic Journal* over the last three years. These articles were written primarily for readers with some Japanese business experience but nonetheless still somewhat baffled by Japanese business practices found nowhere else.

Therefore, I tried to direct the readers' attention to some of my specific experiences in Japan, and then to relate these experiences to generalizations about Japanese management.

The first part, "The Silent Smile," deals with the general background of management in Japan. The second part, "Management Styles—East and West," deals with more specific aspects of doing business in Japan, and the third part, "Different Culture, Different Problems," deals with problems faced by expatriate managers in Japan. In the last part, "Management Myopia or a Bold Approach?" I have tried to contrast some important aspects of management East and West.

I firmly believe that any businessman engaged in international business should be sensitive enough to appreciate the different sets of management assumptions in other countries. During my fifteen years of consulting for the top management of foreign companies, I have observed that executive behavior is often based on preconceived misconceptions (prejudices, if you will) about the business environment; the validity of such assumptions rarely questioned. Yet executives engaged in international business should always ask themselves whether the value system developed at home is also valid in a foreign country.

Management problems in international business often arise from executive misperceptions, and the real problem is often not the decisions themselves but the way they are made.

While I was writing these articles about doing business in Japan, I was also concerned with businessmen who are engaged in business elsewhere, and I hope that the information presented will be helpful not only for understanding Japanese business practices but also for casting new light on personal factors in multinational management. For instance, a recurrent theme which appears time and again is the importance of continuity and the need to instill a sense of security and camaraderie among Japanese employees. Nevertheless, I am well aware that, while this is an important criterion for success in Japan, it may not be valid in a different environment having a different set of social and cultural norms.

In writing these articles, I have called on the help of many friends and colleagues. In addition to those whose names are mentioned in the articles, I should particularly like to thank Koichi Nonaka (Representative Director and Executive Vice President of Stanhome Ltd.), Chisato Uematsu (Japan Personnel Manager, Philips Industrial Development and Consultant Co., Ltd.), Shoichi Osakatani (Chief Coordinator for International Corporate Relations, Mitsubishi Motors Corporation), Kunio Okabe (Deputy General Manager, Corporate Planning-International Department, Nippon Steel Corporation), Mitsuya Goto (General Manager, Public Affairs, International Division, Nissan Motor Co., Ltd.), Masaaki Hirokane (Manager, Planning Development Department, Warner-Pioneer Corporation), Reinosuke Hara (Director, Daini Seikosha Co., Ltd.), Masaaki Matsushita (President, Shaklee Japan K.K.), and Fred Uleman (President, Japan Research Inc.) for assisting me in writing these articles.

John Condon, former Professor of Communications at International Christian University, first brought my attention to the interesting experiment in international communications mentioned at the very beginning of "Silent Smile," and I have since discovered that this experiment was conceived by Professor Lambert at Waseda University in the 1960s.

My thanks go to Kiyoshi Kawahito (Associate Professor at Middle Tennessee State University) for permission to quote from his very informative paper. I also wish to thank Susumu

Ohara of *Japan Economic Journal* for his unending support in writing these articles, and Ichiro Fukao (Deputy Director, Publication Department) and Yoshiro Yamada of *Nihon Keizai Shimbun* for making this publication possible.

As a result of writing for "News from Hotel Okura," I have had the chance to become better acquainted with the Okura management, and I have been most impressed. My sincere gratitude goes to Iwajiro Noda (Chairman), Yasuo Hashimoto (Director), and Mutsumi Fujigasaki of the Hotel Okura for having given me the opportunity to write for their pages.

Last but not least, my thanks to my secretary, Noriko Igarashi, and to Reiko Kondo for their assistance in sorting out materials and typing my untidy manuscripts.

Masaaki Imai

(September 1980)

CONTENTS

● PART III————
Different Culture, Different Problems

● PART IV————
Management Myopia or a Bold Approach?

PART I

The Silent Smile

1
The Silent Smile

●People from different cultural backgrounds may draw
entirely different conclusions from the same situation.

男 The Kanji character at left means "man" or "male." As
you can see, it is made up of two parts: the character 田 meaning paddy field and the character 力 meaning power or strength.
Therefore, the character 男 symbolizes a man working in the
paddy field or carrying the field on his shoulders. Yet assuming
that this man is busily working in the paddy field, which way
do you think he is moving? To the right or to the left? Take a
moment and make your choice before you read on.

If you are an American, chances are that you will say that he
is moving to the right. On the other hand, nine out of ten
Japanese will say that he is moving to the left. There may be
many plausible reasons for this difference. For instance, in
writing this character, the Japanese usually end with the last
stroke applying leftward pressure, and this may be one of the
reasons why many Japanese feel that the man is moving toward
the left. To an American, however, the same last stroke ap-

parently looks like a prop pushing the man to the right. While the Japanese feel that this man is gently walking to the left, Americans may even detect a certain defiance as he fights against the pressure from the right.

The point of this exercise is to illustrate that people with different cultural backgrounds may arrive at entirely different conclusions even when they look at the same scene. It is, therefore, possible for expatriates in Japan to look at the behavior of the Japanese people and to arrive at conclusions which are far divorced from reality.

Lafcadio Hearn, an American writer (born of an Irish father and a Greek mother) who came to Japan in the early Meiji period and later became a naturalized Japanese, reported the story of a maid who did not come to work for a few days. When she showed up next, she was carrying an urn and said that her husband had suddenly died, that she had had to go through the funeral, and that the urn contained the bones of her late husband. She pointed to the urn and said, "This is my husband" and laughed. Such behavior may strike many people as gross, weird, and even "inhuman." Fortunately, Lafcadio Hearn knew better. As he interpreted her behavior, she was saying, "I am sorry I have missed work for so long, but this is why. I am also sorry and embarrassed to have to bother you with such an unpleasant story. However, I am smiling to cover up my embarrassment and to tell you that I am not asking for your sympathy."

In negotiating with a Japanese businessman, it is possible for an expatriate to misinterpret the cues. For instance, the Japanese businessman is usually much less assertive than his Western counterpart. Given the apparent Japanese receptiveness, the expatriate may even feel that the more he pushes, the more the other side will yield. This is not true, and it thus comes as a shock to the expatriate businessman when negotiations that he thought he was "winning" abruptly end in failure.

If a Japanese businessman makes a comment in the course of negotiations which has a negative tone to it, this comment should be taken seriously no matter how hesitatingly it was made. Even when the Japanese businessman has to be negative, he tries to balance it by accentuating some hopeful and positive aspects. This has become almost a ritual, and it has been elevated to an art in Japanese conversation. However, the point being stressed is the negative one, and not the positive side. After all, there is no need to balance out a positive comment, and thus if a comment has both positive and negative overtones, it should be obvious which one is the point and which one is camouflage. Yet all too often, the inexperienced expatriate in this ritual takes the positive side seriously, and almost entirely neglects the negative point which the Japanese executive wished to get across. There is an endless list of such cliches:

I like your proposition very much, and we thank you for your kind offer, but under the circumstances . . . .
I think it's a wonderful idea, but . . . .
We are quite interested in your proposition, but . . . .
We need more time to study your proposition.
Maybe we should discuss this some other time.

It may still be possible for the expatriate to push the deal through, but the important thing is what happens afterwards. If the Japanese side takes a genuine interest in the proposition, they will usually follow it up with prompt action. However, if they are not really sold on the idea, nothing will happen. It is thus possible to win the argument but lose the commitment.

Given a long tradition of valuing harmony and collectiveness, and abhorring dissidence as sticking out like a sore thumb, it is not the Japanese way to take constant exception and argue. Winning an argument is not even regarded as a sign of virility.

There is a Japanese phrase, *menju-fukuhai*, which means to comply outwardly but to revolt inwardly. This often happens (particularly between a boss and his subordinate), because people tend to give up verbal communication halfway. While the boss appears to have won the argument, his subordinate has not really bought the idea.

Even when a Japanese businessman does not agree, he seldom voices a rebuttal right away. And when he does make a counter-argument, it is phrased with great consideration and non-aggressiveness. A businessman used to the way business is done in the U.S. or Europe may think that his proposition has been accepted when it was not explicitly rejected. Nothing could be further from the truth in Japan.

We are often facetious about the Japanese delegates who attend international conferences and abide by the so-called 3S rule of Smile, Silence, and Sleep. Underlying this 3S rule is the feeling that the formal conference presentation is not as important as what happens after the meeting. I suspect that there is a similar 2S rule in many business negotiations (hopefully excluding sleep), but an expatriate should learn that smiles and silence on the part of the Japanese executive do not always mean positive acceptance.

(*November* 1978)

2
16 Ways to Avoid Saying No

● *The most typical way to say no is to say yes.*

One is not supposed to say "no" in Japan. It is rude, impolite, uncivilized, demoralizing, and might hurt the other person's feelings. Saying no is a cardinal sin in Japan. One has to be tactful and diplomatic in the resort to euphemism and non-verbal communication in conveying a negative message.

Foreign businessmen who are unable to interpret this Japanese behavior at the conference table are condemned to a bitter and costly experience in terms of unfulfilled expectations, disappointment, and executive time wasted.

In my book *Never Take Yes for an Answer** I wrote that "yes" does not always mean yes in Japan, that there are some 16 ways to avoid saying no, and that it is not in the Japanese tradition to call a spade a spade. Since then, many readers have asked me to elaborate on these different ways to say no without coming right out and saying it.

The first, and perhaps most typical, way to imply no is to say yes and then to follow this with an explanation which may last half an hour and which, in effect, means no. One has to be very attentive to catch this, since the tone of the response is affirmative throughout the conversation. Forget about such

---

*The Simul Press, Tokyo, 1975.

window-dressing interjections as "But of course," "By all means," or "Quite right," and do not be misled by the affirmative tone. Concentrate on what is being said and find out if you can get a firm commitment for the next step.

The second way to imply no is to be so vague, ambiguous, and evasive in reply that the other side loses track of what the issue was. Sending out contradictory signals, Japanese businessmen hope that the other side will get the hint and take the initiative in calling the talks off.

The third way is simply not to answer the question and to leave the matter unattended. The postponement of a decision on a pending issue is tantamount to saying no, and this is a tactic often employed by government officials. Other ways include abruptly changing the subject, criticizing the other party, or suddenly assuming a highly apologetic tone.

A foreign businessman may suddenly find himself derailed in the midst of his sales talk to a Japanese customer.

Foreign businessman: Therefore, our products meet your requirements 100%. How soon do you think you can place an order?

Japanese businessman: Did you see the *sumo* wrestling last night?

FB: Well. . . . Yes, I did. But back to our discussion, when would it be convenient . . . ?

JB: What did you think of Jessie Takamiyama? Wasn't he terrific?

There is no way the poor foreign businessman is going to get these discussions back on the track, and the best thing would be for him to realize that they have been derailed on purpose.

I once escorted an American company president on a visit

to a large Japanese company which he wanted to persuade to adopt a very ambitious scheme. Among the executives from the Japanese company present at the meeting, we noticed that the executive in charge of liaison on the project kept his eyes closed throughout the discussion, and it was not certain whether he was asleep, meditating, or what. But it was clear that he was not listening. As expected, the project never materialized.

It is said that in the West, when a boss (or a teacher) is confronted with a difficult question to which he does not have an answer, he often resorts to the following tactic. First he says, "That is a very good question," and then he looks the other person squarely in the eye and says, "What do you think?" Thus his authority is affirmed and his reputation for wisdom remains untarnished.

The Japanese boss is no less tactful. Where there is a substantial gap in social status between the two parties and the superior does not wish to answer outright, he may say, "I will consider it." He merely postpones the decision until later, and it is strictly up to him whether he follows through or not. Or he may suddenly get angry with the other person and start criticizing him. This is another way of saying no. Conversely, when he is in a good humor, he may laugh it off and pass the whole subject off as a joke.

As for the subordinate who is asked an embarrassing question and does not wish to parade his ignorance, he usually scratches his head and emits a long drawn-out "Saaah. . . ." which translates as "Beats me."

When the boss calls in an employee and asks him to conduct a survey by such and such a date and the employee says unenthusiastically, "I will do what I can," the boss knows that he cannot count on him. The report will never be submitted.

Another format which is employed by a thoughtful and taciturn businessman is to fold his arms, gaze at a spot on the ceiling with a grimace, and mumble something like, "Mmmm . . . that . . . may . . . not . . . be . . . so . . . easy."

In the typical Japanese communication, one has to be able to hear between the lines. Just as in a *haiku* poem, what is left unsaid is just as important as what is said. The Japanese side is saying, "I am sending you all the necessary messages and signals because it would be an embarrassment for me to have to say no and for you to be rejected. I hope you will please understand what I mean."

When a foreign visitor is not certain whether he is getting a negative signal or not, it might not be a bad idea to ask a simple question that can be answered negatively with "yes" such as "Do you think we should call off the negotiation?" or "Do you think maybe another meeting is not necessary?" At least it would save the Japanese businessman the embarrassment of having to say no.

(*December* 1979)

3
Honne and Tatemae

●Tatemae *is what you are supposed to say,* *and* honne *what you want to say.*

In a recent interview with a Japanese newspaper editor, Henry Kissinger said that he had found Japanese politicians and government officials to have two distinct formats of sounding out public opinion—one the formal negotiations and the other more personalized; and that what was left unsaid was often more important than what was said. He also stated that the Japanese social and cultural heritage makes us reluctant either to give the impression that a particular individual was instrumental in making a decision or to want to take the credit for a specific decision.

Kissinger went on to say that it is quite difficult for an American to find out whom he should be dealing with. Although Japan has achieved outstanding development since 1945, it is difficult to attribute this success to any particular individual. Rather, it has been the Japanese people collectively who have achieved this phenomenal success. In the case of China, for instance, it is possible to mention such names as Chou En-lai, but there is no single outstanding leader in Japan.

I suspect that Kissinger acquired the art of private and personalized negotiations with Japanese politicians in one of the secluded Japanese restaurants so favored for such get-togethers. In any event, he touched upon some basic features of the Japanese character, and his observations are valid not only in dealing with Japanese politicians but also in dealing with businessmen.

It is said that a Japanese expresses his opinion in two ways: "*honne*" and "*tatemae.*" *Honne* is one's real intentions, and *tatemae* is the "facade" of what one is expected to say given his position and role. Some Japanese laws, rules, and regulations are not spelled out very precisely, leaving their interpretation and enforcement to the responsible government officials. This is why administrative guidance is such an important government tool in dealing with business. From the standpoint of implementing a law, the provisions of the law themselves may not be as important as how they are interpreted by the official in charge. Therefore, reading the law alone, no matter how carefully, does not necessarily explain how it applies to a particular case. There is ample room for the official to interpret the law, and this interpretation may change when new cases are added and when circumstances change. Therefore, an executive must find out how the law is interpreted by the official.

When an executive goes to see the government official and has a formal meeting with him at the government office, it is likely that the official will produce the law book, recount the philosophy of the law, and generally explain how it is supposed to apply to the specific case. But the discussion will never go beyond that. Only on a more private basis, at another time and another place after the official has had a chance to become personally acquainted with his caller, can he confide his *honne*, or real intentions.

To get at "*honne*," we not only need to have an informal and private occasion, but we also need a strong "emotional" participation. This is when we depart from "reason" and move into the area of the heart. In Japanese, this opening up to each other is called opening the belly, never opening the brain. It is not so much logical articulation as it is gut vibrations.

Were reason all, one should be able to discover the other party's real intentions no matter when or where the discussion took place. Yet in heart-to-heart communications requiring a strong emotional involvement, both the time and place are very important—and the official negotiating table is certainly not the right place nor the first visit the right time. It is important that the two parties first establish a close rapport which makes it possible for them to communicate heart-to-heart.

Therefore, this communication of *honne* may often be done as a personal favor, and this is why certain information is very difficult for Western expatriates in Japan to come by. This is also why intermediaries who have the confidence of both sides are often used.

Honne is the time when one forgets all the lofty theories and gets down to the nitty-gritty. However, when the two parties are not close enough, it runs the risk of miscommunication, since heart-to-heart communication does not need to resort to lengthy verbal explanations but takes place through casual remarks, hints, suggestions, and even gestures. It is easy to miss these signals unless the prerequisite rapport is there.

In emphasizing the distinction between *honne* and *tatemae*, it may be instructive to recall the story of a researcher who was at a government office collecting some industrial data. Although it was not classified information, the official was reluctant to give it out, since it was not meant to be made public at the time. Instead, he said, "I am not in a position to provide you with this information. However, as a researcher you are free to pick papers up off the floor and look at them if you wish." So saying, he casually dropped the sheet of paper with the statistics on it and left the room for a few minutes. In this case, the *tatemae* was that he could not disclose the information to an outsider, but his *honne* was that he wanted to be helpful.

(*June* 1978)

4

Sharing the Blame

● *Why were these people held responsible*
for something they did not do?

For two weeks each August, practically all Japanese are
glued in front of their TV sets. The Japanese are known to be
very fond of baseball, and August is the time for the finals in
the National Senior High School Baseball Championship
Tournament at Koshien Stadium. These Koshien play-offs bring
together the forty-nine teams which won their local tournaments, involving a total of 3,100 high school teams throughout
the country. Each one of the forty-nine teams competing at
Koshien is expected to do its best for the greater glory of the
prefecture which it represents, and "Koshien" is every high
school baseball player's dream.

In 1978, however, there were three high school baseball
teams, two of which were considered likely to win a berth at
Koshien, which refrained from participating in the local tournaments.

The reason? Some members of the team were charged with
assault and battery. In one case, those charged were not even
baseball team members but were members of the cheering
squad. In another case, one sophomore player had developed
temporary hearing problems after being hazed by some junior
upperclassmen.

The fact that some baseball players or cheerleaders were

Koshien: every high school baseball player's dream
[Kyodo Photo]

involved in such incidents was enough to bring disgrace and shame to the entire high school, and the school authorities voluntarily decided not only to refrain from participating in this year's tournament but also to forego all official games this year as a sign of penitence and as an occasion for the players to reflect upon their moral standards.

Why is it that the other people had to be held responsible for something they did not do? This is the Japanese practice of collective responsibility. It is not uncommon in Japan for the entire group to undergo penance when some of the group have acted improperly.

When I was in grade school, the teacher often told the whole class to stay after school and made us mop the corridors when a few people did not do what they were told during class.

Many Japanese adults who have been in the military, particularly in the army during the Second World War, still remember the days when they were held collectively responsible

15

for something someone else had done. For instance, if one person was found missing some personal gear during the regular barracks inspections, the whole squad would be told to line up and would be slapped in the face, sometimes with the sole of a slipper. Many new recruits had to go through a similar process before they were accepted as seasoned veterans. Although this was supposedly done in order to impress upon people that one mistake during combat could be fatal for all, the concept of collective responsibility was the main underlying factor.

During Japan's feudal era, when a person was convicted of a serious crime, his whole family was often punished along with him. For instance, the Tokugawa Shogunate strictly prohibited the Japanese people from going abroad, and violation of this rule meant death both for the individual and for his family. Thus during the early days of the Tokugawa period, fishermen who drifted while fishing in the Pacific and arrived in the U.S. would not give their names for fear of jeopardizing their families.

The phenomenon of collective responsibility among businessmen is, therefore, nothing new in Japan. For example, when the year-end financial accounting shows a grave deficit, it is not uncommon for management to share the responsibility by accepting reduced salaries and bonuses. In such a case, all directors and managers from the president on down to middle management accept salary and bonus reductions, even though it may be only one particular department that is responsible for the sudden decline in profits. When the corporate profits suffer, it becomes difficult for management to give in to union wage demands, but when management has accepted pay cuts, it is likewise difficult for the union to push too hard for higher wages.

The other side of the coin of collective responsibility is that individual responsibility is not pursued when something goes wrong. In the vast majority of cases, it is not clear who should be really held responsible for the mistake. Of course, the person responsible may know that he is to blame, but the responsibility is shared equally by the group as a whole.

In Japan, the ultimate in responsible corporate behavior may be to hand in one's letter of resignation. Thus a person wishing to implement new changes against the will of his superiors is said to do so with his resignation letter in his pocket so that he can take the responsibility should worst come to worst.

Management attitudes toward employee responsibility are one outstanding difference between Japanese companies and Western companies doing business in Japan. In the Western company, there can be no misunderstanding as to who is responsible. If someone cannot be found to hold responsible, the Western attitude will be to start a witch hunt until someone is found. However, this singling out of one responsible individual runs counter to the strong sense of group identity and participation which is characteristic of Japanese company employees.

(*July* 1978)

5
Time Will Tell

●*He was content to be patient and to wait for others to appreciate his talents.*

I used to have the privilege of visiting the late Shoji Hamada, a modern Japanese pottery master, at his home in Mashiko,

Pottery by Shoji Hamada

Tochigi Prefecture. He never failed to be most gracious and considerate toward his guests. He would show us around his kilns, show some of his latest work as well as various art pieces which he had collected from all over the world, and sit with us and talk for hours around the sooty *kotatsu* hearth in the old farmhouse.

As his lifelong friend Bernard Leach of St. Ives, Great Britain, once said, Shoji Hamada was a well-rounded man in looks as well as personality, and his well-roundness was evident in his work.

The tea cups that they used for themselves as well as for their guests had such a beautiful texture and coloring that they appeared to be just as precious as those great Hamada master-pieces displayed in museums. Although I had similar tea cups from his kiln which I used at home, they never acquired the same depth. So one day I asked if I could take those used cups home, but Hamada gently declined and said that our cups would acquire the same luster over the years if we would keep on using them. However, there was a big difference between the way we used the cups and the way they were used in Mashiko.

At Hamada's home, they would use the tea cups all day, not only for themselves, but also for their many guests, and after each use the cups would be vigorously scrubbed with a scrub brush. These tea cups are thick, heavy, and strong, and can stand a country scrubbing. After a countless number of such scrubbings, these ordinary tea cups developed an artistic texture.

Whenever he entertained guests, he would spend most of the day with them and would work late at night at his potter's wheel or glazing pots. Since I knew that his family was concerned about his health, I often had to restrain myself from visiting him for fear of stealing too much of his time during his later years.

It is reported that Hamada one day found that the hair from his dog's back was ideal for his brush. After that, the careful observer would sometimes notice the dog running around with a balding back. When he was not using his hair brush, Hamada used a spoon to glaze plates, a technique which he developed. Once a visitor who came to his shop and saw him spoon-glaze a bowl in a fraction of a second exclaimed, "What simple work it is!" Hamada only smiled and said, "Please remember that it took me 60 years to do this."

Since Hamada never signed his work, some people were concerned that imitators might appear and claim that their work was Hamada's. To this, he would say that only the very best of his work would be remembered as Hamada's and that his poorer work would be passed on to posterity as that of his imitators; while the very best of his imitator's work would be passed on as Hamada's. I believe that what he meant was that he did not have to explain the value of his own work since it spoke for itself and that it was up to posterity to appreciate it. Just as the worth of the tea cups was enhanced by their repeated use and scrubbing, the greatness of a work of art is something that is observed, appreciated, and even created by those who come into contact with it.

When he made this comment, he was also speaking of himself. In other words, he was saying that he did not have to sell or defend himself. Let others make that decision. If it takes several generations, why worry? Great man that he was, Hamada was content to be patient and to wait for others to take the initiative in appreciating him.

It is in the Japanese tradition to wait and wait until one's true value is noticed and appreciated. To clamor for immediate approval is regarded as shallow. The ability to wait is also an important prerequisite for people in positions of leadership, for it gives people time to pause and reflect, and events time to take their natural course.

In the lifetime employment system, employee evaluations are done over a long span of time, and management does not need to hurry in assessing someone. As a result, a Japanese employee tends to be more passive about selling himself, since he feels that it is up to his boss to recognize his contribution. He is ready to wait.

When people are confident of their own worth, they are more concerned with pleasing themselves than with pleasing others. As a result, they strive to meet their own high standards and pay only incidental attention to lesser demands. Of course, this is not unique to Japan, but it should be remembered as an important facet of Japanese behavior.

The same thing is also true of other great men elsewhere, as I was reminded on a recent visit to England. It seems Christopher Wren built the Windsor town hall with an elongated roof extending over the porch a few hundred years ago. Since the roof did not have supporting columns, the townspeople began to be worried, and the town council told him to build additional columns to support the roof. This he did. It was not until 200 years later, when the plaster between the columns and the ceiling gradually came off, that the townspeople realized that the architect had built those columns only to satisfy the townspeople. The columns did not support the ceiling at all; he had filled the top of each column with brittle plaster and sand. Today, the porch columns stand confident of their own beauty, stopping just short of the ceiling. Hamada would have appreciated the beauty of it.

(*December* 1978)

6

A Personal Leavening

● *Japanese want a boss who is exacting in business matters but warm-hearted on the personal level.*

Surveys of Japanese businessmen reveal that most want a boss who is exacting in business conduct but warm-hearted on the personal level. Thus it appears that a boss who is very strict in seeing that his subordinates perform their duties but at the same time can touch his subordinates' heartstrings and give them the feeling that their boss cares about them is most successful in securing their whole-hearted loyalty. However, with the disappearance of strong father figures and the advent of the "permissive" society, there seem to be fewer and fewer bosses who can meet these requirements.

Konosuke Matsushita, the founder of the Matsushita group, is famous in Japan as the living personification of management. Starting from scratch, he developed his small shop into one of the largest industrial groups in Japan, including such companies as Matsushita Electric Industrial Co., Ltd. and Matsushita Electric Works, Ltd. In particular, he is famous for his skill at training and developing his people, and selecting the right person for the right position.

A former plant manager at Matsushita Electric Industrial recalls his encounter with Matsushita many years ago when he made an important policy change without consulting Matsushita first. Of course, Matsushita soon found out, and late one cold winter night he got a call to come to see Matsushita at once. Matsushita was sitting by the coal stove chatting with a relative, but as soon as the plant manager showed up, he began to shout. He was so infuriated that he would not calm down even when the relative tried to mediate. Shouting and ranting at the manager, Matsushita repeatedly knocked at the stove with an iron poker, so often that the tip of the poker was bent. When Matsushita noticed it, he thrust the poker at the manager and shouted, "Straighten this out!" What with the hot stove and the intense, almost violent, berating, the poor manager could not stand the pressure any longer and fainted from fright.

The next morning, shortly before the plant started operating, the telephone rang and the manager picked it up to hear Matsushita's familiar voice.

"'Morning! Nothing special here. Everything all right there? Great. Carry on."

At this, his miserable feelings of the previous night were immediately dispelled. This is just the sort of "extra" consideration that pleases and motivates subordinates.

I suspect that in the West when a boss is mad enough at an employee to bend the tip of an iron poker, his first reaction would be to say, "You're fired!" and to throw the man out on his ear right then and there. In Japan, this does not happen, since the man is employed for life. When a Japanese manager feels that an employee does not have the potential for improving himself, he does not even shout at him. He simply shuts him out.

Hideo Yoshida, the late president of Dentsu, the largest advertising agency in the world, was famous for his aggressiveness and his unique way of dealing with people.

It was Yoshida, for example, who wrote the famous ten mottos of business for Dentsu employees, including:

- Create your own business and do not wait until it comes to you.
- Tackle the bigger job. A smaller job makes you smaller.
- Don't be afraid of friction. Friction nurtures progress and positiveness.
- Attempt the harder job. Progress is when it is done.
- Once you tackle a task, don't give up until your objective is achieved, even if it costs you your life.

Sometimes he shouted at meetings and even knocked his subordinates' heads together when he got excited. He didn't say, "You're fired!" but he often said, "Don't bother coming to work tomorrow!" Of course, his employees came to work as if nothing had happened. However, from time to time, there were less-confident employees who took this at face value, and such people found it extremely difficult to work for Yoshida. Yet during Yoshida's 15-year presidency immediately following the Second World War, he introduced such new concepts as account executives and creative systems in the old-fashioned

Japanese advertising business, and laid the foundations for Dentsu to become the world's No. 1 advertising company.

A certain young Dentsu employee, whom we shall call N.B., was an expert in the traditional Japanese sport of *kyudo* (archery). A few days after he joined Dentsu, there was an all-Japan *kyudo* tournament, and he took an unauthorized leave to participate in the tournament, which he won. The next morning, the newspapers carried the story of his win. Since he had been away from work without leave, he was naturally more than a little apprehensive when he was told to report to the president's office. Yet instead of raking him over the coals, Yoshida asked him about *kyudo* and the tournament. When their talk was over, Yoshida produced a new American-made suit and told him to take it with him and wear it. As a young man who was just starting out his business career, he was most gratified to have this new suit, although he found it a bit too big for him. Thereafter, he was told to report to the president's office shortly before Christmas each year, and each time he was given a new suit. This pleasant ritual lasted until N.B. was promoted to departmental manager.

Yoshida was famous for giving presents to people he liked. Apparently N.B. was not the only person to get a suit from the boss. It is said that Yoshida personally gave away a total of 1,000 sets of golf clubs to his media associates and clients, including those who had never played golf before, and this contributed considerably to the subsequent "golf boom" in Japan. Incidentally, it should be added that Yoshida developed one of the leading golf courses near Tokyo and was its Board Chairman for many years.

(*April* 1979)

7
Paring the Rolls

Generating rumors that the company is in much worse shape than it really is can be good mangement strategy.

One of the leading Japanese telecommunications companies, with about 13,000 employees, recently took the drastic measure of paring its personnel rolls by about 10%. First, the company provided lucrative incentives to encourage employees to seek voluntary early retirement. When they found that only about 1,000 employees, or 7.7%, had signed up for early retirement, they resorted to the so-called discharge by nomination for the rest of their quota. In doing this, they singled out some 300 employees for individual interviews with the management followed by letters of discharge explaining the unavoidable circumstances which had forced the management to take this regrettable step. In doing this, management had, of course, conferred with the union and obtained prior approval of this modus operandi.

While most people who were discharged by nomination took it calmly, a few who could not resign themselves to resigning formed a group and filed suit, claiming that the discharges were unfair and discriminatory. Several discharged bachelors still occupy rooms in the company's suburban bachelors' dormitory and are battling on with management for reinstatement to their old positions in the company. Other discharged employees have refused to accept the retirement allowances and are considering a court appeal. So far, it is safe to say that the courts have generally favored the employees.

Given the extreme difficulty of discharging employees in Japan, management usually goes well out of its way to seek an amicable parting. For example, most Japanese companies that have been hit by the prolonged business slowdown have formed such departments as "personnel advisory office," "job advisory office," and "special task room." Whatever their names, these offices all have the same task: to place redundant employees outside of the company. The job is not easy. In the first place, most of their redundant employees are in the older age bracket, and there are few job openings for these people.

Because of lifetime employment and seniority-based wages, these older people automatically fall into the "executive" and "managerial" category. On the other hand, most job openings now available are clerical, if not manual, and there are few openings which require executive and managerial capabilities.

Second, most of these redundant people come from depressed industries, and whatever professional or technical expertise they have is related specifically to that industry and is thus itself redundant, since the entire industry is in a slump.

Third, these older people have been receiving seniority-based compensation with their companies but will have to accept job-based compensation if they seek employment elsewhere. It is safe to say that the ordinary clerical type of work that is available in smaller companies will not pay much more than ¥150,000/month on average, while these people may have been getting paid twice that before being discharged.

It is said that there is a 7-5-3 rule which holds for military personnel retiring from Japan's Self-Defense Forces. In looking for employment in the private sector, the retiring officers and other military personnel hope that the new job will pay 70% of their former salaries. The personnel officers assisting with this relocation hope that they can find something that will pay about 50% of the SDF income. However, when the retirees finally settle into their new jobs, they find that they pay orly about 30% of what they used to get. But they accept the jobs anyway, since they are also getting government pensions.

For all of these reasons, it is quite natural that employees should think twice before they quit a company, particularly if the company is a well-established one, even though the business may be having rough going. In the case of the company mentioned earlier, it is reported that only about half of the 1,300 people who retired found new jobs within a few months of quitting.

Most Japanese unions are "enterprise" unions, organized by and for employees of that one company. In this, the unions share a common fate with management and are often sympathetic with the management cause at critical moments.

The union at a leading machinery company recently announced a plan to establish a special fund to assist union members who may be asked to quit the company in the future. The object is not to use the fund to fight back against management proposals but rather to assist people who have accepted management's urgings and quit the company.

Under this plan, up to ¥50,000 will be paid to help tide over a former union member who has taken voluntary retirement and quit the company, and if he later accepts a job elsewhere at a lower wage, the money will be used to compensate him for his sacrifice.

In the case of the Tokyo Metropolitan Government, those who are "tapped" for retirement are offered a special bonus which amounts to 50% of the normal retirement allowance. However, not many civil servants are willing to take early retirement even so.

It is no wonder that Japanese management is very cautious about firing redundant employees. A friend of mine, president of a medium-sized company, once told me how he went about getting rid of his redundant employees at the time of the 1973–74 oil shock. First, he had to get several board members who had been with the company from his father's time to quit. This proved an excellent way to get rid of the old guard. Second, he cut the number of managerial posts in half. Third, he generated rumors within the company which gave the impression that the company was in much worse shape than it really was. When the worried employees consulted the union, the union leadership, which was in on the plan and agreed that the company had to let some employees go in order to survive, suggested that they would be wise to find employment elsewhere. Thus the company found that about one-third of the employees voluntarily submitted their resignations in the wake of the oil crisis, and the company was able to save tens of millions of yen which would otherwise have had to be paid to encourage early retirement under pressure.

However, such tactics do not always work, since it is usually the more capable and ambitious employees who quit early in times of distress, leaving the company with only the less ambitious and mediocre people who had no prospects elsewhere and opted for safety within familiar surroundings.

(*January* 1979)

8

Easing Him Out

●Forcing an individual to take the "responsibility" for something in Japan requires politics, diplomacy, and patience.

When the Liberal Democratic Party (LDP) made an unexpectedly poor showing in the October 1979 general election, the opposition factions within the party set up a chorus of criticism directed at Prime Minister Masayoshi Ohira. Ohira had decided to dissolve the Diet and call a general election, expecting that the LDP would gain a comfortable absolute majority of 256, and hoping the party might win the 271 seats it needs to have a majority in all of the Lower House committees.

When the votes were counted, however, the LDP ended up with only 248 seats, one less than it had before the election and eight short of an absolute majority.

Since the Prime Minister did not have to dissolve the Diet and call an election, and should not have done so unless he was confident that the LDP would win, his critics demanded that he "take the responsibility" for the election's outcome.

In Japan, this taking responsibility is often synonymous with resignation for people in public life. However, Ohira insisted that his "true responsibility" lay in fulfilling his campaign promises, and that this meant he had to stay in office. The opposing faction leaders were not convinced, and one faction leader seeking to break the impasse suggested that a consultative body be organized in the party to discuss the Prime Minister's responsibility. This Ohira rejected.

Later, it was suggested that the entire matter be left to the LDP vice president, who would hear out opinions within the party and then make a compromise decision which would be binding on all parties concerned. Although the vice president visited with faction leaders and tried to form a consensus, Ohira maintained that only he knew best where his responsibilities lay.

After many weeks of bickering, this issue of whether or not to hold the Prime Minister accountable for the poor election showing came to a temporary end when a majority of the LDP Dietmen voted to give Ohira a second term as Prime Minister. This entire episode has been very interesting, not only as political theater but for what it says about the way responsibility is understood in Japan.

In the first place, what was it that the Prime Minister was to be held responsible for? Except for some pre-election wishful thinking that the LDP would pick up additional seats in the Diet, there was no clear-cut demarcation between victory and defeat. The LDP lost one seat in the Diet. Although everybody called it a serious setback for the LDP, was it really a defeat? When the target itself is unclear, the responsibility for not achieving the target must also be unclear and subjective. It therefore followed that the solution had to be "situational," since there was no well-defined frame of reference against which to judge the outcome.

Second, there was a long series of consultations involving the good offices of well-meaning third parties mediating among the interested parties before the final showdown.

Finally, the decision whether or not to quit was mostly left to Ohira, and the most the others could do was to resort to moral suasion. This is typical. The Japanese generally dislike forcing someone to take the ultimate responsibility, and would much rather work out a solution of moral suasion and compromise.

Responsibility is assigned among the top management of Japanese companies in much the same way. It is not uncommon for the president to remain in office for years even when the company is losing money. Just as a poor election showing was not sufficient to force Ohira out, neither is a disappointing bottom line the only criterion for evaluating a company's performance. A change of management takes place only when the company's very survival is endangered or when the supporting financial institutions demand it.

The members of the board are mainly operating officers of the company, and the president is both the de facto chairman of the board and the chief executive officer. Therefore, the board is not in a position to fire its own president. Whether he should resign or not is mostly left to his own discretion. This is why in Japan some presidents remain in office for years even in the face of deteriorating performance. On the other hand, Japan's system of lifelong employment makes it impossible for the president to fire his own executives. Typical rules of employment specify that an employee may be dismissed in Japan only for one of the following reasons:

1. Failure to satisfactorily perform his duties due to incurable mental or physical illness.
2. Such poor performance and attendance that he is deemed unfit for the performance of his duties.
3. A scaling-down of the business operation for some unavoidable reason.

Nowhere is it stated that an employee may be dismissed for a mediocre performance. Since there is no job description, there are no criteria against which to judge his performance. What is more, Japan's collective decision-making makes it difficult to pin the responsibility on a single individual and to hold him responsible for a poor performance. Therefore, the boss is unable to say, "Your duty was to do such and such, but you did not do it, so you are fired." Even were management willing to fire an employee, he has broad defenses to fall back upon, and management must justify its decision impeccably. There have been many court cases which have supported the employee in his contention that the reasons for the dismissal were inadequate.

There are a number of steps which must be taken before an employee can be dismissed outright. Typical rules of employment stipulate the following gradations in management sanctions.

1. Give the employee a letter of warning.
2. Get a letter from the employee acknowledging his misconduct.
3. Dock the employee's salary a limited amount.
4. Suspend the employee from service without pay.
5. Demote the employee.
6. Urge the employee to take voluntary retirement.
7. Fire the employee.

Forcing an individual to take his "responsibility" in Japan obviously requires much politics, diplomacy, and patience.

(*November* 1979)

9

The Right Job for the Man

● *Management is more concerned with who should get the job than with what the job is.*

It has often been pointed out that lifetime employment and seniority-based wages have made Japanese management unique.

In Japan, when one begins his career with a company immediately after graduation, there is the expectation that he will work for that company until he reaches retirement age and that his position in the company will automatically improve and his salary will be raised commensurately each year. As a result, both employer and employee tend to look at each other with a long-term perspective spanning the employee's entire working life. This employment environment has given rise to a number of personnel administration practices which are distinctly different from those in Western countries. Let me illustrate such differences in personnel administration between Japan and the U.S.

To begin with, Japanese management places the main emphasis on recruiting new graduates, usually in April each year, while in the U.S. more emphasis is placed on mid-career recruiting programs throughout the year. In Japan, management tends to look at the individual from the standpoint of his overall contribution. Thus Japanese management tends to evaluate the employee's performance on a long-term basis, while U.S.

management tends to evaluate personnel on a short-term basis.

In Japan, remuneration is incidental to the person. He receives the same compensation no matter what position he holds in the company. Therefore, monetary incentives do not play a major role in Japan. Rather, the employee is motivated by being assigned to a more challenging position. In the U.S., remuneration is tied to the job, and a given job carries the same compensation no matter who holds it. Therefore, changing jobs is the fastest way to earn more money.

Finally, since Japanese management is interested in the employee's overall capabilities, it has much more leeway in assigning new tasks to its employees. Because there is an underlying belief that a capable and trustworthy employee will probably do any job well, management is more concerned in selecting a new man for a position with *who* should get the job than with *what* the job is. In other words, whether or not the man has sufficient expertise for the new job is a secondary consideration as long as the man has a proven record of success in some field or other.

In selecting a new person for a position in the U.S., the job requirements come first and the man who best meets these requirements is selected. If a qualified person is not available within the company, they will try to find someone from outside. The main concern is to fill the job vacancy. There is a set of precise requirements called a job description, and they try to find someone who fits the mold. The man's worth to the company is directly proportional to the degree that he fits whatever job they have for him.

In Japan, however, an executive may easily be appointed to a position for which he has little or no expertise. But if he is the right choice, he will become an expert at the new job within a few months. Management recognizes this and does not expect him to be effective right away. Since he grows into the job, management is willing to give him time to grow. Thus Japanese management matches manpower resources to jobs with more freedom and encourages people to develop skills in new and different fields.

I find Western managers to be less tolerant and flexible in regard to this man-job relationship. Instead, Western managers seem to adhere to a philosophy that the man is there to do his job—his current job here and now—and a man of proven capability is seldom transferred to an entirely different and new field.

For instance, foreign companies in Japan looking for a personnel manager usually insist that the candidate should have so many years of experience as personnel manager. They do not want to consider someone who may lack experience as a personnel manager but has proved very capable in other fields and may have the potential to do the job. On the other hand, when a Japanese company selects an employee to be sent abroad, for instance, his linguistic expertise may not even be one of the more important qualifications, since they expect him to make an effort to develop the language in due time.

I believe that one way for management to increase its overall manpower effectiveness is to reevaluate its personnel, not from the standpoint of how well their current qualifications fit their current jobs but from the standpoint of their overall potential and what new assignments they might be given for further development.

If management will take an unbiased look at the man-job relations in the company, they may well find a vast reservoir of untapped potential. Similarly, if management is willing to hire someone from outside who may be very capable overall but lacks the specific experiences to prepare him for the particular slot, they may well find that they have a larger pool of excellent resources available outside of the company.

In order to do this, however, management must be ready to wait for the man to grow. It must be mature enough to give him the chance to make mistakes and tolerant enough to see him through in the long run. Assigning a man an entirely new job could well be just the challenge he needs to motivate him to develop his full potential.

I do recognize the pitfalls in doing this. For one, the man may prove to be totally incompetent in the new job. Also, starting from scratch and hoping that the new man will learn the job soon is ill-advised when "timing" is an important factor. Nor is it wise to assign a highly technical or professional job to someone who lacks the professional background. However, such a transfer of personnel is not only possible but even beneficial in most management positions.

This is thus one area in which Japanese-style management may be helpful to Western managers. In this respect, I should like to make the following suggestion.

When you have a vacancy, forget about things like job requirements and the job description. Forget about insisting on MBAs and all that fancy certification from the big-name universities. Take a fresh look at your own people and the people you interview. Review their performance and potential. Give them new assignments not on the basis of the narrow job description but on the basis of their overall potential.

After all, a man cannot grow *up* to expectations unless they are set higher than he already is.

(*May* 1979)

PART II

*Management Styles–
East and West*

1

Hygienic Sales

● *A Japanese manager considers his contract in terms*
of customer relations.

The sales manager for a record company recently told me
about his experience with the owner of a small record store in
a small town. The man appeared to be very taciturn and
difficult to get along with, and salesmen did not like to call on
him. Among other things, he kept on paying in ninety-day
sight promissory notes when most stores were paying in cash.
One day, the sales manager paid a courtesy call on him and,
noticing a plastic model of a Zero fighter plane in the corner
of his office, turned the conversation to Zero fighters and
what great planes they were during the Second World War. At
this, the proprietor brightened up and said that he himself had
been a Zero fighter pilot.

The proprietor was so pleased with the conversation that, as
the sales manager was leaving the room, he pulled out his
check book and wrote a check for the total balance due right
there. And he has been paying in cash ever since.

Zero fighter: the weak point in his defenses [Kyodo Photo]

A few months later, when the record company sponsored a "Saturday Night Fever Disco Party" in his town, the ex-pilot volunteered to host it and was the very first person out on the dance floor. There is no doubt that the sales manager knew how to get on the old fighter pilot's good side.

According to Frederick Herzberg's theory of motivation, there are two factors which are equally important in maintaining worker morale: the motivator and the hygienic factor. The motivator includes the job itself and such job-related factors as the challenge, the prospects for promotion, recognition, and the sense of accomplishment which are instrumental in improving a person's morale and making him more enthusiastic.

The other factor, the hygienic factor, includes such factors as the work environment, wages, and human relations; and unless the hygienic factor is satisfactory, worker morale will be low even if there is enough motivator present. In other words, the hygienic factor may be likened to the foundation upon which the true motivator can be built.

I believe this is analogous to doing business in Japan. Very simply, the hygienic factor is much more important in Japan than in the West. In sales, for instance, the product, the quality and quantity to be sold, the price, delivery dates, the terms of payment, and other "hard" aspects may be likened to the motivator. They are business-related factors and important prerequisites to consummating the sale. However, there is also the hygienic factor of what may be called customer relations.

Of course, maintaining good customer relations is an important prerequisite in conducting business anywhere in the world, but it is especially important in Japan. While a Western manager considers his customer relations in terms of the contract, a Japanese manager considers his contract in terms of his customer relations. In other words, the contract may be flexibly interpreted in view of the importance of maintaining the customer's goodwill, and there may be times when the Japanese company is willing to go beyond the call of duty as specified in the contract.

Thus, from the standpoint of the Western manager who thinks that the customer should naturally deal with whoever has the better product and offers better terms, business in Japan appears to attach undue importance to maintaining good customer relations. On the other side of the coin, however, a little additional effort to maintain good customer relations can produce surprisingly favorable results.

The first "hygienic factor" in conducting business in Japan is to consider customer relations on a long-term basis. When two companies are working together for years, there may be times when one or the other gets the short end of a particular stick. For instance, a new product may not live up to expectations and may have to be withdrawn from the market. In such a case, the retailer expects that the supplier will make an effort to make amends for this some time in the future. It is a give-and-take relationship.

Foreign companies doing business in Japan often fail to establish such a relationship with their customers and, as a result, fail to gain their confidence. Once a business relationship has been established, it is important to try to build ever-stronger ties by constantly attending to those apparent misunderstandings that occur from time to time. For instance, whenever a claim is filed against the supplier, the customer expects the supplier to send a man right away. Such attentiveness is considered a mark of sincerity.

Maintaining frequent personal contacts with the customer is another important hygienic factor. For instance, a salesman is expected to call on customers more often than is really justified, since the frequency of his visits is regarded as a measure of his sincerity.

"*Gobusata-shimashita*" is often heard when someone is calling on a customer in Japan, either in person or on the phone. Basically it means "I'm sorry to be out of touch for so long," and the salesman means it. He is sincerely sorry to have been "out of sight" for so long, and he hopes the other party has not put him "out of mind" as a result.

This is why so many courtesy calls are needed. There may be times when a telephone call suffices, but the smart businessman takes the time to visit his customers in person. Moreover, these constant personal contacts are enriched by exchanges of gifts (*o-chugen* in summer and *o-seibo* in winter) and seasons' greeting cards.

(*July* 1979)

2

The Salesman Cometh

●Who would dare write "baby-sitting" in the sales report?

A typical Japanese salesman's report on a sales call, if he ever prepares one, may read:

"I visited one of our important customers this afternoon, although I had no particular business to discuss with him. I talked briefly with his wife and played with their five-year-old boy. I also gave the boy some toys before coming back to the office. I believe that the time I spent was quite productive."

Nonsense? He may be doing just the right thing.

Hiroshi Torigoye, President of Bausch & Lomb-Japan, recalls the difficulties they encountered in developing new accounts when they first started selling Bausch & Lomb's soft contact lenses. Here is the story of how one of his salesmen finally succeeded in winning over an influential eye doctor in one small city.

On his first visit to the eye doctor, even before he had a chance to explain about Bausch & Lomb, the doctor gently brushed him off, saying, "We have been using your optical instruments for years, so we know that they are good. But as far as soft contact lenses are concerned, we are perfectly satisfied with the conventional contact lenses and there is no need for us to use your lenses." Since this was his first visit to this clinic, he decided to hang around for a while and see how it was run.

He talked to several nurses (paramedical assistants) when they were not too busy and got to know them. He also talked to the doctor's wife and tried to find out more about her husband. (In Japan, the management of a clinic is usually left to the doctor's wife.)

The next day he went back to the clinic again and hung around to watch what people did and to familiarize himself with their work. The doctor was indeed quite busy, and appeared to have little time to spare. Later, he went into the kitchen and listened to the doctor's wife discourse for a while on her favorite subject—cooking. He also kept her son company when he got back from kindergarten, and took him to the toy store to pick out a new toy.

The wife, of course, was very pleased with this well-meaning baby-sitter, and in the course of the conversation she suggested, "Since my husband doesn't have any time to listen to you during office hours, why don't you come back again after dinner?" He was more than willing, and came calling again that evening.

This time, the doctor was in his *yukata*, relaxed, and sipping *sake*. He had apparently been briefed by his wife, and gladly took the time to listen to the salesman's presentation. When it was over, the doctor said, "You know, I can't use the new products on our patients right away, but why don't we try them on our assistants first and see what happens?"

The next (third) day, the salesman went about fitting Soft-lenses for several assistants, all the time providing a running professional commentary for the doctor. The reactions of the assistants were all favorable.

At long last, this intensive three-day sales campaign was crowned when he finally made a sale to the doctor.

Actually, the phrase "making a sale" is misleading in this account. In Japan, making a sale like this often means going through a very difficult and complicated decision-making process, whether it be with customers, retailers, or department stores. The marketing manager for one Japanese consumer goods company once suggested to me that, in view of the difficulty of closing the deal and the balance of power between the buyer and seller, it might more appropriately be called "getting a license."

Says Torigoye, "Our customers look at how frequently our salesmen call to judge whether or not we really want their business. If our salesman calls more often than our competitor's, he is regarded as more "sincere." For the same reason, I am also expected to call on our more important customers a few times a year."

No wonder then that a salesman often calls on a clinic just to show the flag—even if there is no business to discuss. Only after many such calls, and only after he has gotten to know everybody in the clinic, is he accepted as a member of the "family." Only then can he establish a long-lasting rapport. Once he is "part of the family," the doctor may take a personal interest in the salesman's life, and may even help him find a wife through an arranged marriage.

Torigoye recalls how a competitor lost an account when a customer moved to new and larger quarters. For an eye doctor, opening a new clinic is the experience of a lifetime, and for someone who has been invited to the opening ceremony to fail to show up is not only bad form, but may be taken as a personal affront to the doctor. On this particular occasion, it happened that there were railway strikes the day before the opening ceremony, which prevented Torigoye's competitor from getting there, while Torigoye drove all the way from Tokyo to keep his promise. It was a mark of his sincerity, and soon Bausch & Lomb had both companies' business with this eye doctor.

In the United States, management would typically request the salesman to set up objectives for his sales calls and to report afterwards on whether or not these objectives have been fulfilled. This kind of logic often has no place in Japan. For instance, who would dare write "baby-sitting" under the "objectives to be accomplished" in the sales report? The Japanese are generally "situation-oriented," and the objectives of the call themselves may be subject to change depending on the customer reaction. If the customer does not appear eager to discuss business, the salesman may turn the talk to other subjects such as hobbies and come back without having even put in a good word for the product.

According to modern business management theory, a manager's job is to delegate work and manage his subordinates. If a sales manager starts to call on customers instead of concentrating on managing his salesmen, he is not doing his job properly. In Japan, however, customers often expect the sales manager—and even the president of the company—to make courtesy calls a few times a year. Being generous with your time is often a mark of sincerity and a measure of how earnestly the company wishes to do business in Japan—a point which many expatriate managers find baffling.

(*June* 1979)

3

The Radio in the Refrigerator

● *A Japanese manager sometimes finds emotional means the most effective problem solver.*

In the late 1950s, Sony was having difficulty in marketing its radios in the six prefectures of the Tohoku region (northeastern Honshu). Sony radios were then sold through Panasonic's retail chain, and it looked as though sales had peaked out and were gradually falling off. Isao Moriguchi, then product manager for Sony radios, was faced with a need to do something to boost sales in the Tohoku region.

One day, while going over the monthly sales report from a field salesman in Akita Prefecture, he noticed the following footnote: "I visited a small retailer in Akita who told me that he had conducted a small experiment on the Sony radio and the Panasonic radio and found the Panasonic radio to perform much better."

After reading this report, Moriguchi phoned the salesman and found that the "experiment" had been conducted by putting the radios in an empty washing machine! He then called up an engineer in the R & D Department and asked if such an experiment could show any difference in the quality and performance of radios. The answer was that it could make *some* difference depending on how the radio is placed in the washing machine, but that the difference was not related to the radio's performance quality. The engineer further suggested that the difference would have been minimal if the experiment had been conducted in a refrigerator because of the space limitations in the refrigerator.

Moreover, R & D also advised that the test would yield no marked difference in performance among different manufacturers' radios but that, if the tester were psychologically ready to favor a particular model, chances are that he would think that model had performed much better.

When the engineer was finished, Moriguchi told him to pack an overnight bag and go to Haneda Airport, where they caught the next flight to Akita. When they got off the plane at Akita Airport, they were met by the field salesman who had prepared the report. Together, they drove to the retailer's shop. It was well past 7:00 at night when they got there. It was a very small mom-and-pop outlet, and the proprietor was first surprised, and then greatly honored and privileged, to have such distinguished visitors come all the way from Tokyo to see him. While he was apologizing for having caused so much trouble with his amateur experiment, the Sony engineer was setting up to replicate the washing machine test and then to do another test with the radios in the refrigerator. As expected, there was no discernible difference; but also as expected the proprietor had been greatly flattered by this visit from Sony and was thus most impressed with how well the Sony radio performed.

After the experiments were over, there were a few rounds of *sake* and then a few more at the proprietor's home. By midnight, they had all become such good friends that it seemed as if they had known each other all their lives.

Moriguchi had known beforehand that there would be a convention of all Panasonic retailers in the Tohoku region in a few days, and this was one of the reasons he had decided to visit this store. Sure enough, within a few days after the convention, every Panasonic retailer in the Tohoku region knew about his visit and the experiment which Sony had conducted. For a small store in an outlying area, this visit from the Sony head office was a once-in-a-lifetime experience, something the proprietor would cherish forever, and he must have told the story to everyone he met at the convention. Apparently, this episode brought Sony personally closer to many retailers, for Sony radio sales in the six Tohoku prefectures jumped about 20% shortly afterward.

It is reported that this proprietor still cherishes the fond memory of Moriguchi's visit and sends him New Year's cards even today. From time to time, he also sends Moriguchi presents such as the famous Akita *sake* to keep up the relationship. For his part, Moriguchi never fails to call on him and have a few drinks together whenever he is in Akita, even though Moriguchi is now Executive Director of Brain Inc. and has nothing to do with radio sales.

In differentiating between Japanese and Westerners, it is sometimes pointed out that the Japanese are *emotionally* oriented and Westerners *intellectually* oriented. Thus a Japanese manager sometimes finds emotional means more effective in solving a particular problem.

For example, the Moriguchi story may appear incomprehensible and even insane from an "intellectual" standpoint. If a Western product manager came in and asked for permission to fly off to some out-of-the-way city with an engineer to see a small-time retailer who had done some stupid test in a washing machine so that they could do the same inconclusive test in a refrigerator instead, an *intellectual* boss would likely suggest he go soak his head. If the visit with the retailer had turned out to be futile, how many companies would be ready to pay the expenses? However, whether the above incident made sense from the intellectual point of view or not, the important thing is that it worked! It created personal bonds among the key people involved, and these bonds set the marketing machinery to working.

In one of Tokyo's many suburbs, there are two big stores, one a specialty store selling home appliances and the other a general-merchandise store. Recently, a few days after the specialty store started selling a particular model of electric fans, the general store inserted fliers in the neighborhood newspaper advertising the same electric fans for ¥1,000 less. When the specialty store manager saw this advertisement, he ordered his salesmen to track down the 30 customers who had already bought fans at his store at the higher price. It was not easy, but the salesmen were finally able to find 28 of the 30 customers. The manager then called on each one of them, apologized for having sold the fan at higher price than their competitor, and gave them each a ¥1,000 refund. Most customers had not even known that the same fan was available at a cheaper price, and they appreciated the manager's "sincerity." In fact, it is reported that these customers made additional purchases at this store shortly thereafter which averaged ¥10,000 ($50) per person. Here again, the Japanese "emotional" approach did the job. (Incidentally, what these customers did not know was that the management of the specialty store later filed a claim with the fan supplier and had the supplier pay the difference.)

(*March* 1979)

4
Debt Accounting

●*Feelings of indebtedness accumulate interest.*

The Japanese are said to be very conscious of social differences, and it is supposed to be very difficult to establish a truly equal relationship between people of different backgrounds in Japan. Therefore, excepting those who are very close, such as age-peers working in the same office and/or friends from the same university sports club, a superior-inferior relationship is likely to emerge between people of different backgrounds.

When a person feels indebted for help received, he will naturally express his appreciation or try to repay the kindness in one way or another. Logically, one would assume that once the favor was returned, the ledger would be wiped clean and they would be even again.

Not so in Japan. When one feels greatly indebted to a particular person, his feeling of indebtedness grows over the years! As someone has put it, this "*giri*" or feeling of indebtedness accumulates interest. Moreover, this is compound interest, and the longer one puts off repaying the debt, the more interest accumulates. And the man who does not pay the capital and interest on favors for which he is indebted will be accused of ingratitude.

Thus a man who found his wife with the help of a go-between will feel indebted for that help even after marriage, and will

Go-betweens: part of the entangling web of obligations

show his appreciation by sending gifts to the go-between in June and December every year.

Sometimes, this debtor or creditor position may even be inherited. Stories abound in Japan in which people befriended by a man will band together to help his family after he dies. I personally know of at least one case in which grateful people showed their respect for a man after his death by contributing considerable sums of money to start the man's son in business.

When there is a feeling of indebtedness, it is difficult to maintain an equal relationship between the two parties, no matter how many times the debtor side may have reciprocated the favor. It is not a mathematical relationship. There can be no exact accounting because of the deep-rooted emotional involvement factor. The interest on the debt has to be paid back indefinitely, since it is often impossible to return the psychological debt itself.

It is the same thing with buying and selling. In Japan, selling in a buyers' market is tantamount to begging, just as is buying in a sellers' market. Buyer and seller will never be on an equal footing. Let me dwell on selling in the buyers' market, since it is more common. When a sale has been achieved in a competitive market, the seller feels obliged, and his obligation lingers and grows.

The buyer, knowing that he has done the seller a favor, naturally expects some "interest" aside from the business transaction itself. Therefore, he does not regard the deal as closed just because he has paid for the purchase and the account is closed. This is why Japanese customers often behave tyrannically and make many seemingly unreasonable requests even after they have purchased a particular product or service.

For instance, when a Japanese customer makes a purchase at a department store, she assumes that she can return the merchandise if there is something wrong with it later.

Last winter, I bought some ski wear at a leading Tokyo department store's branch in a winter resort hotel. On the very day I bought it, I took a fall while skiing and tore the ski wear. When I got back to the hotel, I happened to meet the store manager in the lobby and showed him where I had ripped the knee. He said that he was sorry it had torn on the first day out and wanted to do something "to make up for it." Sure enough, they gave me an entirely new outfit. No wonder the prices are so high at that store! This is the kind of "service" people expect of a conscientious store.

When a customer purchases a fur coat at a leading department store, the store may offer to store the coat in its stock room during the first summer free of charge. Consumers expect a wide range of other "free" services from the department store as well, including free delivery.

Japanese consumers are said to be just as fussy as they are demanding. It is reported that when Japanese women shop for fashion wear, the first thing they do is to turn it inside-out, look at the seams, and complain if the stitches are a little out of line—all this even before they find time to admire the pattern or design!

These same customers make a big fuss when they find a little dent in a can of food on display, even though the dent has nothing to do with the quality of the contents. Therefore, dented cans usually find their way into the "loss leader" baskets in the supermarkets. The consumer is indeed king in Japan.

If the consumers are demanding of the department stores, the department stores are no less demanding of their suppliers. In most department stores, goods are sold on consignment, and left-over goods are sent back to the suppliers. In fact, one reason the department stores can be so willing to concede customer complaints and replace defective products is that they can pass the buck to their suppliers. Department stores also ask suppliers to provide their own sales people at the counter. Most sales people you see at the Japanese department stores are paid not by the department store but by the companies that make or supply the products being sold.

It is also difficult to establish an equal relationship in a business deal between two companies, and one side is likely to assume a deferential and yielding posture. To the Western mind, closing a sale means closing the book on that particular sale. Again, this is not so in Japan. Operating in a buyers' market, the seller usually feels obliged to the buyer for having made the purchase, and this sense of indebtedness lingers on.

Therefore, the sales manager for a foreign company in Japan often finds himself caught between two extremes in dealing with customers. The head office in New York or London assumes that the sale represents nothing more or less than an agreement to sell and buy between the two parties. To them, it is strictly a business deal, and there is no obligation except as set forth in the contract. When a deal is closed, it is closed, period. If the buyer thinks of something else later, this is a separate issue and should be dealt with as such.

On the other hand, the Japanese customer expects a variety of "services" from the seller even after the deal has been closed. The Japanese customer expects to collect "interest" on the deal, yet the Western head office's psychological books do not show this interest, and the requests are flatly rejected as unreasonable.

In the Western sense, each deal is a one-shot deal. In Japan, it is not, simply because the seller feels indebted and tries to repay his debt. This is why Japanese businessmen prefer to negotiate with a longer time-frame in mind. Psychologically speaking, one deal is related to another. For instance, the negotiations for the price of a particular product may often be related to the price of another product which is going to be put on the market soon. This is also why "package deals" are preferred by Japanese companies.

When a deal's one-shot nature is overemphasized, management tends to slight its long-term obligations to customers, obligations such as maintenance and prompt parts delivery. Most friction between Japanese and foreign companies doing business in Japan stems from precisely this lack of long-term commitment and flexibility in doing business in Japan.

(*May* 1980)

5
Go to It

*●Leaving room for the other player to take
the initiative sometimes makes for a better game.*

Hideo Otake, holder of the title of *meijin* (master) of the
traditional Japanese game of *go*, recently told me that one of
his favorite games was the one he played against Eio Sakata
during the latest championship matches. According to Otake,
no matter how many moves he made in this particular game, he
felt the boundless expanse of the board was undiminished.

The *go* board is marked with 19 horizontal and vertical lines
such that, since the black and white stones are alternately
placed on the intersections of these lines, there are initially
361 (19^2) points on the board where the first player may
place his first stone. As the game progresses, the board gradually
fills up and there are fewer spots to place the stones, fewer
moves to make, and hence fewer alternatives. In the game
against Sakata, however, Otake apparently felt that their
moves did not exhaust the board and did not have a restrictive
effect on their next moves. In other words, in this particular
game, each player played in such a way as to leave his opponent
a wide range of options and to keep his own strategic freedom of
response.

Unlike chess, which is an individual-centered game in which
the different pieces have different capabilities and winning
is defined as checkmating the opponent's king, *go* is a territory-

Sakata and Otake: the boundless expanse between them
[Nihon Kiin photo]

centered game in which every stone has the same worth and the object is to control more territory than one's opponent, even if it is only a difference of just one point. There are some fundamental rules in the game, but it is basically a simple-ruled game which is difficult to play well. As a result, one resorts to various strategies and tactics in the course of the game.

Although the object is to gain territory, the player who concentrates too early and too much on a specific section of the board will find himself outflanked elsewhere. It is a game of long-range finesse and positioning. Attacks may coalesce from preparations begun more than a dozen spaces away. One move in a remote corner often has a way of activating the entire battlefield. There are also times when one particular move is so direct and straightforward that there is no other alternative but to reply, and this can easily escalate into a series of moves in which both players' moves are determined as direct responses to immediately preceding moves.

I am often struck with how relevant the tactics and strategies of *go* are to doing business with Japanese management. For instance, when one wishes to influence a particular executive within a large Japanese company, it is often more effective to talk to a third party in the expectation that the message will be conveyed to the right person at the right time. An attack on a right-hand corner may well be initiated in the left-hand corner.

This is also why I was so intrigued with Otake's remark, since he was pointing out that every move both contestants made in this particular game was such as to leave the other person the widest possible range of alternatives. Rather than saying, "I have made this move. Your only response is such and such, after which I will . . . ." in a linear progression, it was more like saying, "I will make this move. You can judge for yourself what alternative response is best for you. I shall develop my plans after seeing what you do." In other words, both Otake and Sakata gave each other maximum freedom of choice and did not try to narrow the scope of the battle unnecessarily. Of course, the very placing of stones obviously imposed physical limitations on future moves, but both parties were playing so well that Otake felt the immense expanse of the board no matter how many moves he made. *Go* professionals call this unstructured style "*aite ni te o watasu*" or "letting the other player take the initiative." This initiative can easily be hemmed in, but the more freedom of action both players have, the better the game.

In the game of management also, one has to select the best alternative of many. Sometimes, however, particularly in negotiations, it may happen that, instead of forcing the issue, it is better to let the other side take the first step and then decide what to do in light of that development.

This mention of the Japanese tendency to forego taking the initiative reminds me of another popular axiom among professional *go* players: "Don't look at the sound of your opponent's stone." In other words, if you look only at the sound—which means only at the latest stone played instead of its implications for the total game—your thinking will be rigidly concentrated on how to respond to that particular move. However, if you always remember the relationships across the whole board and think of the various alternatives given the current situation, the best move may be not to respond to a particular move, but to place your stone somewhere else. However, 99 out of 100 amateur *go* players forget this admonition and think only in terms of how to respond to their opponent's latest move. Therefore, since they only "look at the sound" and neglect to consider what it means in regard to the entire board, they lack the important strategic option of not responding directly to a particular move.

In this same vein, Yasuharu Oyama, a master at the Japanese chess-like game of *shogi,* claims to be able to tell which side is winning merely by looking at the wrinkles on the *zabuton* cushions they sit on. The one who is winning usually sits back on his cushion and surveys the entire board carefully, while the one who is losing usually hunches over the board and concentrates on particular battlegrounds. Therefore, when they go for lunch, the winner's cushion is wrinkled on the back edge and the loser's on the front edge.

Given this background, it is little wonder negotiations with a Japanese businessman (or politician) often look as though the Japanese side is playing *go.* To begin with, the Japanese side waits for the other side to make the first move. Impatient, the Western side takes a vigorous initiative and comes up with a comprehensive set of requests and propositions. It is only when this initiative has been put forth that the Japanese side begins to decide what course of action to adopt in response. From the standpoint of the Western individual, such a reaction may appear too weak, too passive, and/or too slow.

What is worse, the Japanese side often fails to respond directly, and the Western side may feel inclined to accuse the Japanese of non-responsiveness and even insincerity, when the fact of the matter is that the Japanese side is sitting back the better to see the entire board rather than watching the latest sound.

This strategy appears to be very common among Japanese politicians in particular, especially when they are unsure of their own positions. Actually, there is no such thing as "their own positions," since their positions are relative to the other side's positions and moves. Using this mindset, their own positions will be formulated only in response to the demands imposed by the other side.

Japanese politicians have often been accused, both domestically and internationally, of having no principles and being non-committal and indecisive. One word often used to describe their posture is *tamamushi-iro* or "iridescent," since the color looks different depending on where you are looking from. However, this very iridescence may well be their position, since its ambiguity, by enabling them to delay any definitive declaration, allows them to choose the solution that best fits the circumstances.

Japanese executives are said to have three hobbies: *go, kouta* ballads, and golf. Most large Japanese companies have *go* clubs and stage in-house tournaments. There are even tournaments among leading companies. It is easy to see that *go* may have had a strong impact upon Japanese executive strategy formation.

Shigeo Nagano, president of the Japan Chamber of Commerce & Industry, and also director and honorary chairman of Nippon Steel Corporation, is known to be very fond of *go*. In fact, he holds the highest amateur rank. On one of his recent trips to London as leader of a Japanese businessmen's mission, it is reported that he kept up a session of *go* in the plane all the way from Narita to Moscow and then to London, until his opponent, also an avid player, finally could take it no longer and pleaded for an end.

While the Japanese may tend to overemphasize the advantage of letting the other side take the initiative and keeping a wide range of alternatives open, it seems to me that Westerners tend to overemphasize the advantage of taking the initiative and hemming the other party in. The meeting place of East and West surely must be somewhere between the two extremes. Perhaps more Westerners should be encouraged to play the game of *go*. If you are interested, stop by my office. There is a board right beside my desk.

(February 1980)

6
Management Styles–East and West

● *In Japan, management and employees are one and the same.*

Kentucky Fried Chicken is reported to taste different from store to store in Japan. As in other countries, Kentucky Fried

Chicken Japan uses the same store facade, the same color combination, chickens from the same farm, the same frying oil and sauce, and the same utensils in accordance with the same instruction manual. And yet, somehow, different stores' products taste different, and there are reportedly several gourmets who will take the extra trouble to visit a store which offers a "better" taste.

This is inconceivable to the Western mind. In fact, the Kentucky Fried Chicken management says that the same recipe is used in Japan as in the United States and that it is impossible for Japanese employees to make any changes.

However, it is true that there are many similar incidents in Japan. For instance, it is also reported that the Sapporo "rahmen" noodles taste different from store to store in the Dosanko franchise chain. As franchisees, all the stores are supposed to have identical menus and price lists. Yet they seldom do. One would imagine that the management of a franchise chain would make doubly sure that manuals are followed closely and that all outlets offer identical products and services. Maybe so somewhere else.

In Japan, however, the people working at these stores apparently do not follow the instructions closely. Instead, they innovate and try to improve on the recipes, which is why things taste different from store to store.

This story may serve as a clue to understanding the differences in managerial styles between Japan and the West. In the West, the manuals or instruction books provided to salesmen, engineers, and accountants are often as thick as the telephone directory. The idea is that the instructions must be thorough, methodological, and "fool-proof." Moreover, they presuppose the existence of people who will willingly follow such "fool-proof" instructions.

One expert sales manager once told me that there was no need for lengthy sales manuals in Japan—all he needed was a single sheet of paper outlining the salesman's work. Once this is spelled out, it is up to each salesman to work out his own way of doing the job most effectively. It would only be demoralizing for the sales manager to instruct the salesmen in minute detail and to expect them to follow these instructions blindly. In other words, in Japan it is much more effective to set the worker's overall objective and then let him work out the details by himself.

I believe that this difference is accounted for by Japan's homogeneity and uniformly high level of education. The United States, for example, is by comparison a nation of people from many races, many of whom have had only a minimum level of education, who are willing to follow "fool-proof" instructions and to do as they are told.

As a result, the role of management in the West is often that of managing a group of poorly educated and badly motivated people. Here, the difference between manager and managed is distinct. The manager gives instructions and motivates workers, who are essentially followers. They need a "fool-proof" approach.

In Japan, on the other hand, management and employees are one and the same, at least psychologically. By virtue of seniority-based promotion and lifetime employment, the employee sees himself as a likely candidate for the managerial ranks sometime in the future. Psychologically speaking, he is already a member of the management when he joins the company. Because he develops a strong identity with the company, he wishes to participate. Instead of being told everything he has to do, he wishes to work out the details of his own work on his own initiative. This accounts for the big difference in managerial styles between Japan and the West. Seen from Japan, foreign companies overburdening their salesmen, accountants, or engineers with too many instructions may be doing the most demoralizing thing they possibly could.

The distinguishing features of Japanese management are said to be its emphasis on paternalism and collectivism and the resultant system of lifetime employment, seniority wages, and enterprise unions.

Therefore, it takes special skill to motivate Japanese employees. For instance, improving morale by providing individual incentives does not work in Japan. There are many cases where the management has tried to introduce individual incentive plans for salesmen—and failed. It seems that the Japanese employee derives his greatest satisfaction from being a comfortable member of a group, and he does not like the prospect of sticking out like a sore thumb among his peers. If he receives a special offer of financial reward for his outstanding work, chances are that he will turn it down since he is concerned that this may also "buy" him the resentment of his fellow workers. Management is aware of this, and is thus more anxious to improve the morale of the group as a whole than to reward an individual at the risk of losing the support of the rest.

Thus, the divide-and-rule doctrine does not work in Japanese companies, and the tactic of playing one employee against another usually yields poor results. It is much more effective for management to work out some kind of group incentives and to try to motivate the group as a whole.

Coming back to the issue of the franchise chain, one might grant this Japanese ambition to improve the product and still argue that the franchisees are legally bound to follow the procedures and manuals provided by the franchiser.

As seen in the recent revision of the sugar contract with the Australians, the Japanese people seem to believe that an agreement, even after it has been signed, is subject to change if new circumstances arise. In fact, while the contract in the Western sense is categorical and all-inclusive, a Japanese contract often includes a clause to the effect that both parties to the contract agree to reconsider things should unforeseen circumstances arise. This is considered acceptable because of the belief that revision will be feasible at a later date as long as there is a spirit of mutual trust at the time of signing, and it may be a manifestation of "*amae*" on both sides.

Japanese management has been sometimes called management by *omikoshi* or portable shrine. You never know who the leader is, and there may be some who are just jogging along not doing any work, but everyone is very happy being anonymous but enthusiastic carriers of the shrine.

The whole system of personnel administration in Japan is geared to providing high morale for the group as a whole. Seniority-based wages, employee outings, field days, vacation houses, and more are all provided in order to strengthen employee identification with the company and with their fellow workers. Thus while American management tends to feature rugged individualism, togetherness is the conspicuous feature of management in Japan.

Another aspect of management style which appears to be quite different in Japan concerns the decision-making process and the way goals are decided upon. It has been pointed out that Japanese decisions are worked out by middle managers first and then go up to the top management for approval. While such a process is very time-consuming, the decision comes back to the middle managers again for implementation, and since these people have participated in formulating the

Omikoshi: hard to tell who is doing the work

plan, they all understand its implications and it is put into effect fairly smoothly.

In this connection, I should like to add one small observation concerning the significance of goals to the Japanese.

In Japan, the process of arriving at the goal is often more important than the goal itself. Sometimes, the goal may not be appropriate; it may even be unrealistic. But this does not matter, since the main concern is the process of its formulation and not necessarily its accomplishment.

An old essay by Kenko Yoshida, a Buddhist priest of several hundred years ago, tells the story of a man who wanted to become a Buddhist priest. In those days a priest was required to give sermons in the neighboring villages and the man who was not wealthy enough to ride in a carriage had to ride on horseback. So this particular man set himself to learning how to ride. He also knew that he would have to learn how to drink *sake* and sing folk songs well, since he expected that *sake* would be served and that he would be asked to sing after his sermons were over. By the time he had become an expert rider, a well-seasoned *sake* drinker, and a good folk-song singer, he had missed the opportunity of becoming a Buddhist priest. Yet who knows what he really wanted to accomplish!

In the collective system that exists in Japanese companies, setting the goal is a must, whether it is appropriate or not, for it is only with the common goal that all employees can work together and draw up plans to achieve the goal.

(*November* 1977)

7

Blowing a Muted Trumpet

●*Silence is silver, if not golden.*

After the recent Cabinet reshuffle, a new minister said at his first press conference, "I am not at all sure I am qualified to do my job, but the Prime Minister asked me, so I had no choice but to accept."

A Westerner hearing this remark might ask himself, "If he does not think he can do the job, why did the Prime Minister appoint him—and why did he accept the appointment?" Of course, the new Cabinet Minister was appointed because he was more than qualified for the job. At times, Japanese can be extremely humble and self-deprecating, but no one is fooled by such comments.

In the West, the word "presentation" has a special meaning. There is the "presentation" of a new advertising plan to the client. There is the "presentation" of the sales forecast and a proposed budget to the boss. And there is the "presentation" in order to impress others with oneself's worth. Seizing upon every opportunity, the Western businessman has to show how expert he is. He has to sell himself at cocktail parties, at business meetings, and, of course, at press conferences.

In Japan, there is not this same compulsion to sell oneself. A typical Japanese *tatami* guest room (*o-zashiki*) has just one piece of art displayed in the *tokonoma* even though the host may have a substantial collection of art pieces. Instead of displaying all of them on every wall and corner of the room, the Japanese host prefers to show only one special treasure, although he will be only too happy to show other items if asked.

Similarly, the Japanese individual does not feel that he has to blow his own trumpet too ostentatiously. The feeling is that if he is capable, his performance should show it, so why advertise?

It is said that French executives often try to "outsmart" others in a meeting. Here, one has to seize every opportunity in order to test one's wit. When a meeting is held in Japan, there is a strong tendency for everyone to agree, and it is considered bad form to take exception to the prevailing views.

Of course, this does not mean that everyone thinks alike.

It often happens one Japanese executive may be opposed to a proposal while the others are in favor of it. In such cases, the dissident will most probably sit still and defer to the majority without a strong show of opposition, later drowning his frustrations at a nearby bar.

On the other hand, one's contribution in a Western company appears to be based upon the extent to which he participated in the decision-making process, regardless of whether his views prevailed or not. In other words, sitting mute is clearly a minus at the Western conference, while silence is still silver, if not golden, in the typical Japanese mindset. Many Japanese executives sit silent throughout the conference. Nobody thinks the worse of them for that. They are like oxygen: their views may not be visible, but they are making a positive contribution nonetheless.

Today, Japanese employees working for American companies are finding it to their advantage to be articulate, to speak out, and to have a definite yes or no opinion on every issue.

In communicating with his Japanese subordinates, the Western manager often looks for cues for evaluating them. These cues may include a confident and trustworthy appearance, quickness in responding to the manager's requests, an eagerness to be helpful, a quickness of mind, an ability to come up with a prompt answer on the spot, and a willingness to speak up clearly and decisively on every issue which comes up.

Unfortunately, most of these cues are not in the Japanese tradition. When a Japanese subordinate is promoted, the Western manager expects him to say, "Sure, I can do it." But instead the man says, "I am not at all confident I can do the job well . . . ." He looks forlorn at the promotion! While the Western manager wants his subordinates to reach out and to participate more actively, the Japanese employee is afraid that he may be infringing or getting "out of place."

These different approaches are often most evident at the board meetings of joint-venture companies in Japan. It is reported that at one company the Japanese directors are only too eager to terminate the meeting as soon as possible without any overt "confrontation." The Japanese directors appear to have an aversion to discussing "problems" at board meetings. The Japanese directors remain mute in the presence of the president, who usually presides at the meeting, since they report to him in the daily course of affairs anyway, and only the American directors speak out at most meetings. In most cases, it is believed that board meetings are held merely to confirm what has already been discussed informally, and that the informal relationship between the two partners is much more important and effective in managing the company than are these perfunctory board meetings.

It appears that the Japanese company requires a total personal commitment and involvement while the Western company recognizes the diversified facets of personal life. For instance, in a typical Japanese company, the executive tries to use his total personality, and not just his work, to gain his boss's full support. Once such a comfortable relationship is established, such minor mistakes, misunderstandings, or friction as may occur from time to time do not pose serious problems. The important thing between the boss and his subordinate is to try to build a comfortable personal dependence and commitment. Therefore, the superior will usually think twice before expressing strong disapproval or criticism of his subordinate's work, since such disapproval might be taken as a rejection of the relationship itself.

On the other hand, business is business and friendship is friendship for many Western executives. They think that they can be sharply critical of another person's work and still maintain a friendly relationship outside of the office. In Japan, however, scathing criticism will often be taken as a sign that the Westerner is negating the relationship of trust that has developed between them.

Thus the Japanese executive must have the conviction, or at least the feeling, that he is totally trusted by his boss, and without this conviction it is difficult for him to make the total commitment necessary to do a good job. The Japanese executive does not easily differentiate between his private self and his public self. A Chinese proverb which was very popular among the Japanese *samurai* years ago read: A man will gladly surrender his life for one who "understands" him.

In a way, the boss-subordinate relationship may be likened to the relationship between husband and wife. Just as the Japanese husband does not have to constantly tell his wife he loves her, nor will the Japanese couple quarrel violently or get divorced as often as the Western couple. Once the marital relationship of trust and reliance has been formed, it is unassumingly nurtured in the assumption of its totality.

Totality is the key word here. The Western boss who expects to maintain social conviviality in the face of office conflict is in for a rude shock, and just as rude a shock awaits the Western manager who tries to form a closer personal relationship with his Japanese subordinates yet neglects to make the effort to develop similar trust in the office. Either way, the lopsidedness leaves the Western executive open to Japanese charges of artificiality or hypocrisy.

(*December* 1977)

8

Changing Horses

●*Let's have a man-to-man talk in the sauna bath.*

One afternoon in the spring of 1970, Teruyuki Yamazaki, president of Yamazaki Machinery Works, a machine tool manufacturer near Nagoya City, was having his third interview with Naoe Fukumura, a 32-year-old engineer. At that time, Yamazaki was seriously studying the feasibility of going into the NC machine tool field and badly needed someone to head their new R & D department.

In his search, Yamazaki had been directed to Fukumura, then working as an R & D engineer on NC machine tools for another company. Although Fukumura was interested in Yamazaki's proposition, he had to overcome several hurdles before he made up his mind. In the first place, like most Japanese executives, he had spent his entire career with only one company, and this would be the first time he changed jobs. If he decided to join Yamazaki, he would also have to move to Nagoya. For years he had lived by the shore so that he could go yachting, and moving to Nagoya would also mean giving up yachting. Nor was his wife very eager to move with their two young children. It was a momentous decision, and there were several relatives that he wanted to consult before he made it.

Thus, although president Yamazaki had been telling him all afternoon about his role in the company's future plans, Fukumura had not been "sold" on the idea and was unable to bring himself to say yes yet. Suddenly, he realized that it was getting dark. Since he had to take the train back to Tokyo, he thought that it was about time to leave and said, "I still don't know. Let me sleep on it and give you an answer next time."

However, from experience, Yamazaki knew that there would be no next time. It was now or never. So he said, "Now that I have told you all about our company and your role, let's have a man-to-man talk. Let's bare our souls and talk candidly." With this, Yamazaki took Fukumura to a sauna bath in downtown Nagoya where they sat sweating and talking while the steam rolled around them.

Fukumura was greatly moved at this effort to win him over. Here was the president of a busy company, who had spent all afternoon with him, taking him to the sauna bath so they could continue their discussion. That evening, he made up his mind to join Yamazaki.

In 1970, conventional machine tools accounted for almost all of the Yamazaki product line. Today, conventional tools account for less than 10% of the company's business. Today, Yamazaki Machinery Works, Ltd. has become Japan's leading manufacturer of NC machine tools, and it is also very strong in the export market. Unlike most other Japanese companies, Yamazaki does not owe the banks anything. Moreover, debt-free Yamazaki has manufacturing plants in the U.S., Belgium, West Germany, and other countries, and trades not only with the West but with the Communist bloc as well. With about 1,400 employees, Yamazaki boasts annual sales of ¥50 billion.

In 1977, the Society of Mechanical Engineers awarded a special citation to Yamazaki's R & D group, headed by Fukumura, for the development of the YMS-30, "a total machinery system based on an entirely new concept of the machining center." Another highlight in Fukumura's life came when he was promoted to the Board of Directors last year. Asked if he was glad he decided to switch to Yamazaki, Fukumura said, "Ever since joining Yamazaki, I have been so busy in developmental work that, to be quite frank, I haven't even had time to wonder whether I was wise to change jobs."

An increasing number of Japanese executives are making such mid-career changes, although they may not make their decisions in the sauna bath.

During the last thirteen years, the Cambridge Corporation, Japan's first management consulting and recruiting firm, has placed over 3,500 executives and engineers for both Japanese and foreign companies. The executives placed range from top management people such as president or general manager commanding annual salaries of over $100,000 to middle and lower management personnel such as departmental managers, accountants, and sales engineers. Today, not a day goes by without our placing someone somewhere in Japan.

The majority of the Japanese corporations which the Cambridge Corporation has assisted are fast-growing small and medium-sized companies. As may be expected, larger Japanese companies seldom resort to mid-career recruiting programs, since their policy is to hire new graduates and, being long-established, they are under pressure to release, not to hire, middle-aged executives.

During the rapid-growth decades of the 1950s and 1960s, these big companies hired new graduates by the hundreds, and now they are beginning to feel the crunch of these high-cost executives with their seniority-based salaries. So when the personnel managers of the leading Japanese companies come to see us, we know why: they want our help in relocating their middle-aged executives. On the other hand, when the presidents of small and medium-sized companies walk into our office, we know they are there because they need to hire qualified executives.

The American president of an engineering firm once told me that the best way to find out the state of the art with his U.S. competitors is to place an ad for an engineering manager—for he has found that the candidates who show up are surprisingly open about what is going on in their research laboratories.

This probably would not happen in Japan. In the first place, while newspaper want-ads are very popular in Japan also, they are mostly directed at clerical people and salesman. Secondly, the social mores argue against easy mid-career job changes. Most executives have never changed jobs before, and they encounter considerable mental and psychological strain in bidding farewell to the company where they have worked for years, particularly if they are going to join a competitor.

In the West, when an executive makes a career change and assumes a better position in a new company, it is a promotion of sorts, and a raise is almost automatic, since it is assumed that each job has its own price tag.

In Japan, however, the mid-career job change does not always mean a raise, since the price tag is not on the job but on the man, most often meaning on his years of experience. Therefore, it is the challenge of the job itself, the prospects for promotion, and the new company's potential which are the important considerations for a Japanese executive trying to decide whether or not he should job-hop. In this, the top management's commitment, vision, and philosophy often play the decisive role in attracting the better-qualified candidates.

(*March* 1980)

9

Staying Plugged In

● *Admiral Yamamoto sometimes stamped his approval without bothering to read the reports.*

Admiral Isoroku Yamamoto, Commander-in-Chief of the Combined Fleet of the old Imperial Navy during World War II, is reported to have been a very quick decision maker. In fact, there were times when he went over papers, made decisions, and stamped his seal of approval without even bothering to sit down. When papers were forwarded en masse, he sometimes affixed his signet of approval without reading them. At times, the sound of him stamping his approval on papers was almost machine-gun-like in its rapidity. Even though there was so much paperwork that a number of high-ranking officers ended up with sore arms after a busy day at the office, Yamamoto's judgement was rarely wrong, and he never failed to note important issues and even to jot comments where necessary.

One day, an aide watched Yamamoto to see if he could discover the secret to his mode of decision making. Actually, it was rather simple: Yamamoto was not reading the papers—he was reading the men who wrote them. He was accepting or rejecting the papers not by what they said but by who had prepared them. He knew whether the paper was sound or not just by looking at the names affixed to it. He knew what his subordinates were thinking and what they were trying to do, and thus he was able to judge the papers that passed over his desk based upon his appraisal of the men and the situations as they developed within his staff organization.

Obviously, Yamamoto maintained multiple communication channels, both formal and informal, within the Imperial Navy to enable him to evaluate developments and to keep abreast of who was doing what and how. These channels served him well when he was presented with masses of papers to review, for he could draw upon his knowledge of men and situations to assess the papers by assessing the people behind them.

While there are many criteria by which to judge someone, a friend of mine once suggested that the capable executive is one who is able to make four crucial distinctions: (1) between right and wrong, (2) between profitable and unprofitable, (3) between important and unimportant, and (4) between urgent and not urgent. Unless he is able to distinguish between these, it is possible that he is working hard but at the wrong things.

In business as in government, a top executive is faced with a constant flow of information and forced to make decisions on the spot. Very often these decisions will have to be made with very little time for deliberate reflection, consultation, or investigation. In times such as these, the smart executive will have a better basis for wise decision making if he is thoroughly familiar with his people and with the latest developments within his organization.

As a result, multiple channels of communication, both formal and informal, emerge within the corporation to facilitate this decision making. This is especially true in Japan, where employment is "fixed" and people are likely to work for the same organization for years and years. Thus the Japanese manager often finds it faster to go to the right person in the company for information than to wade through the intraoffice memos piled up on his desk. Often these informal communication channels are more convenient and more reliable than the formal ones. The influential manager is the one who has ready sources of information, both formal and informal, within the company. However, these informal information channels are not standard office equipment, they do not come with the job, and they are not easy. Instead, they must be painstakingly cultivated over the years.

A friend of mine was recently appointed director of one of the largest banks in Japan. He was comparatively young for the job, being first-appointed from among his age cohort and even ahead of some people older than he was. This was indeed a conspicuous success in seniority-conscious Japan. When I asked him how he had done it, he only half jokingly told me that it must have been all those after-hours drinking parties the first few years he worked for the bank. As he recalled, he and his colleagues, including his superiors, used to go out drinking after work and seldom got home before midnight. No doubt this was an excellent way to establish those vital personal relationships and to get to know people, and no doubt these after-hours friendships served him well when he wanted to get something done at the office.

Nor is this emphasis on the person unique to business. The late Prime Minister Eisaku Sato, who served longer than any other Prime Minister in Japan's history, was nicknamed "Sato of Personnel" for his skill in making political appointments and juggling people in just the right positions to keep himself on top and everyone else satisfied. Prerequisite to this skill was an intimate knowledge of and sensitive feel for the conflicting interests within the party and the government.

These personal connections are enhanced by shared experiences. Little wonder that the alumni association is frequently cited as among the main advantages of graduation from one of

Japan's better universities. As he moves up, the lucky graduate will find former classmates in influential positions almost everywhere in business, in government, and occasionally in the Diet. If he is involved in a legal suit, he may find friends among the lawyers; and should he be indicted, he may even find he knows one of the prosecutors! Properly cultivated, this fraternity serves as an important informal source of information, and it can readily be expanded beyond former classmates to include graduates from other years at all levels of society.

Lacking such shared experiences, foreign executives in Japan are often cut off from the various informal communication channels which exist. As such, they have to knock on the "front doors" and rely entirely upon formal channels of communication. As such, they get only the official version of something after it has already been decided. How much better to have informal access to information and ideas when a decision is still in the making.

Years ago, the easiest way for someone to establish rapport with his boss was to take a bottle of *sake* and go to visit him at his home after work. Although this ploy has fallen out of favor now that homes are too small to really accommodate visitors, it has been replaced by going out drinking, playing mahjong after work, or playing golf on weekends. And when Japanese businessmen are not drinking, playing mahjong, or golfing together, they will most likely be meeting in small and informal clubs to study and discuss their common concerns.

It is reported that there are as many societies and clubs in New York as there are people, and I am inclined to believe that the same holds true for Tokyo. Although not particularly an "activist," I myself belong to such groups as the "Vision Study Group," "Multinational Corporation Problems Study Group," and "Contemporary Problems Study Group." Each of these groups has its own distinctive membership, but together they are a very varied group including businessmen from different industries, university professors, government officials, journalists, lawyers, Diet members, doctors, and more. It is quite common for the average businessman to belong to several study groups, and to exchange ideas with people from many different backgrounds and disciplines. Recently, that sleepy-eyed American institution, the breakfast meeting, has been adopted as a way to find more time for these unofficial get-togethers. All of these groups serve as important meeting places of the mind and informal channels of communication. Both lubricant and glue, they are part of the unofficial structure that keeps Japan working smoothly.

(*June* 1980)

10

In Dependence

● *Three out of four Japanese children want to remain children.*

Foreign visitors to Japan often observe that Japanese parents discipline their children, particularly their small children, much less than Western parents do. To foreign eyes, the Japanese "laissez-faire" method of child raising is at times so lenient as to border on spoiling the children. However, as Japanese children grow older and become subject to the many social restraints unique to Japan, they find they have less and less freedom to behave as they want; and by the time they are fully grown, they find they have very little freedom in the face of tightly structured social norms. By comparison, children in the West start life severely disciplined and are subject to less and less discipline as they grow older; and by the time they are grown, they find that they are truly free and liberated!

A recent survey conducted by Asahi Tsushin Advertising Agency revealed some interesting differences between Japanese and American school children in this respect. The survey found that while Japanese children study longer than American children, American children spend more time helping their parents. Japanese children have more friends, but most of them are in the same grade in school; whereas American children have fewer friends but from a wider age range.

Japanese children define an adult as someone over twenty, but American children define it as anyone over eighteen. Three out of four Japanese children (74%) want to remain children, while more than half of the American children (55%) want to grow up as fast as possible.

Thus the picture which emerges from this survey is that the Japanese child wishes to remain a child and to enjoy child-like freedom while the American child wants to grow up and to escape the restraints of childhood as soon as possible. Although startling at first, the contrast is made more understandable if we remember that the Japanese children expect to have less and less freedom as they grow older.

Perhaps the best word to describe this Japanese mindset of wishing to remain a child is "dependence." And if a Japanese child wants to remain a child, he may very well indulge in child-like behavior even after he has grown up. Thus is the psychology of dependence retained well after the individual has become an active member of society.

Little wonder, then, that Japanese management is said to be paternalistic, protective, and collective—all of which provide enhanced security and thus satisfy the employees' yearning for a dependence relationship. However, just as a child has to suffer parental restrictions if he wishes to depend upon his parents, so have these employees forfeited a number of important freedoms in order to gain protection within the comfortable embrace of lifelong employment.

For instance, the Japanese employee does not have the freedom to seek a level of income commensurate with his immediate abilities, as the income level is determined according to a fixed formula in the company and not by the individual's own contribution. Thus, it is said that a new graduate joining a company can fairly accurately calculate his total earnings over his entire working life.

Nor does lifelong employment allow employees to choose their own professional careers, since they have to accept the positions assigned them by the personnel department, positions which usually change every two or three years.

This "dependence" phenomemon is also seen in company-to-company relations. At the top are the "big" industry leaders, and below them are the masses of small and medium-sized companies. Indeed, with 99% of all Japanese companies ranked as small and medium-sized, and with these companies employing about half of the total labor population, it has at times been claimed that Japanese industry is sustained by these hundreds of thousands of small and medium-sized companies.

A large Japanese company usually dominates the many suppliers, subcontractors, and sub-subcontractors with whom it does business regularly. The automobile industry is a prime example. Every automobile manufacturer has its own group of companies which manufacture and supply the various automotive parts. Although these companies may formally be no more than parts suppliers, the relationship goes far beyond the normal supplier-purchaser relationship. For one, the suppliers within the "group" are virtually assured of a continuing and long-lasting business relationship with their sponsor company. They are also assured that there will be enough business generated by the group leader to see them through the year.

Sometimes the sponsor company finds that the price its supplier quotes for a particular product is higher than the going market price. But instead of going to another supplier who will offer a more favorable price, the automaker sends technical consultants to the supplier to find out why the price is higher. If it is a problem of not having the technology to do the job efficiently, the purchaser may even provide technical and management consultation to help improve productivity at the supplier firm. In all of this, the sponsor company's main concern is to secure a stable, long-term source of parts at reasonable prices.

Accordingly, once a firm relationship has been established, the sponsor company wants to provide protection to its suppliers so as to facilitate this long-term relationship. The other side of the stability coin is that they abhor any abrupt disruption of the way business is conducted. The cooperating companies often meet with the management of the "sponsor" company to hear about the latest market developments and to learn where the sponsor company is heading. All in all, the cooperating companies find the protective embrace of the sponsor company very comfortable.

On the other hand, there are some drawbacks to this relationship. For instance, the cooperating companies cannot expect to make more than a minimum profit on their business with the sponsor company. Just as the sponsor is quick to help them to improve productivity and to solve their technological problems, it is also quick to step in and to ask for lower prices whenever the supplier is making an "excessive" profit. As a result, the cooperating company often finds itself just slightly above the subsistence level. Since there is little chance of raising prices to the sponsor company, the only alternative is to venture into a new field of business unrelated to the sponsor company. However, this transparent ploy for greater independence can be very risky, and it is the rare subcontractor that will take the plunge. This is even more so when, as often happens, the sponsor has invested in the company, is represented on the board of directors, and has provided executive talent for key posts. In such a situation, suppliers are often little more than subsidiaries of the automobile companies they work for.

Nevertheless, despite the sometimes restrictive nature of the protective relationship, the Japanese psychology of dependence sees this not as a suffocating bear-hug but as a warm, womb-like embrace. Rather than fighting and clawing for independence, Japanese employees and companies alike opt to prolong their childhoods in the warmth of security.

(*July* 1980)

PART III

Different Culture, Different Problems

1

The Japanese Manager—Does He Really Manage?

● *The visiting executive should be careful not to be misled by the managerial title.*

The negotiations had gone along smoothly and now the deal was about to be closed in the Japanese company's executive offices. However, there were still several technical points which needed to be clarified. Citing the urgency of the matter, the visiting American executive vice president insisted that they clear things up immediately and that he had the necessary authorization to approve any changes. When the executive vice president who was negotiating for the Japanese side said that he would have to consult with his colleagues and subordinates, and that the negotiations would therefore have to be recessed until next time, the American visitor found this incredible and insisted that the negotiations be concluded then and there. The negotiations came close to collapsing over whether or not the Japanese executive was empowered to represent his company, the American executive saying at one point, "What I say is final and becomes company policy. I can decide these things by myself. Why can't you?" In part, this argument arose because the American executive did not understand the role of the typical Japanese manager.

The Japanese executive, be he president, vice president, department manager, or section manager, does not have the power to hire and fire his subordinates. In the framework of lifelong employment, the personnel department makes all the preparations for recruiting new graduates each April. Recruiting is usually conducted at the head office, and new employees are hired and deployed throughout the company by the personnel department. As a result, recruiting is rarely conducted at the operational level. Nor do the larger Japanese companies do much mid-career recruiting. Even when a manager recognizes a clear lack of specialized or professional expertise in his department, he is unable to bring qualified people in from outside of the company.

Reassignments within the company are also handled by the personnel department in close consultation with top management, and departmental managers are often unable even to get the people they want for their own departments.

At the same time, nor is the Japanese manager able to fire a person under Japan's system of lifelong employment. The best that he can do with someone who does not measure up is to ask the personnel department to transfer him to another department, but, as might be expected, few departments are willing to take these misfits. Therefore, the typical Japanese executive does not have the power to hire and fire which his Western counterpart often wields to exercise control.

Decision making in the typical Japanese company is often a collective undertaking among all interested managers. For this reason, the manager often acts as a symbol of unification within his organization and assumes the role of coordinator as well as communicator. He has to be guided by his subordinates as well as direct them. He will ask them what he can do to facilitate their work more often than he will tell them what to do. It is said that one of the marks of the smart employee in Japan is that he knows how to manage his boss, since new ideas originating from below are presented to top management for final approval by the department or section chief, and after the idea is approved, it is sent back down to its originators for implementation. Their boss is their representative, and thus lower-level employees must be able to assist and manipulate their boss so that he can influence other managers to their advantage.

To get back to the negotiations I mentioned at the outset, the Japanese manager had to consult with his colleagues and subordinates to find out what the implications of the proposed changes were. Chances are he had not been involved to the extent that he could tell the difference. He may be likened to a high-ranking government political appointee: he may be an amateur in the affairs of his department, but he is in touch with the political power balance and knows what to do to help the people in his department. He also knows the other high-ranking officials and how to influence them. Whenever he acts on behalf of his department, he has the support of his subordinates, who provide him the necessary data and advice.

This is in sharp contrast to the American executive, who is supposed to be thoroughly knowledgeable about the business and technical details under his jurisdiction. If he were not, he would not be there in the first place. Thus it is quite natural that he should pride himself on being able to make negotiating decisions on his own. He may even be inclined to think that anyone who cannot make these decisions is not a real manager. It is not difficult to understand why he should be so frustrated at the "inefficiency" and "incapability" of his Japanese counterpart.

It is safe to say that most Japanese managers are generalists. They are generalists in communication, first of all. They act as communicators between people in different departments, and between their own people and people outside.

In pushing for a specific business decision which requires prompt attention, Western executives sometimes try to push the Japanese company's top management, hoping that they in turn will push the lower-level people. However, this strategy often backfires. Since they are sure they know better, the people at the working level rebel at such pressure from above. Therefore, it may be better to try to establish rapport with people at the working level and to communicate with them directly. Even if this working-level rapport cannot be established, the Western executive should bear in mind that the Japanese manager's power to order, direct, and manage his people may be much more limited than his own.

If the Japanese manager is so handicapped in supervising his people, how can he be held responsible for his department's performance? The answer is that he is often *not* held responsible and that the responsibility is collectively shared by the department as well as by the company.

When Japanese subordinates accompany their boss to a meeting, it is customary for them to stay mute and to let the boss do the talking, even though they may know more about the subject at hand. Even if they recognize that their boss is wrong, they would not want to correct him in the presence of strangers. This gives the foreign visitor the impression that these subordinates have little or no power and may therefore be disregarded. Nothing could be further from the truth. These are the people who are going to make or break the project, and the foreign visitor should never underestimate them, even though they sit mute at the meeting.

As generalists in management, Japanese managers will have held various managerial positions in the company, such as purchasing, sales and marketing, personnel, and general affairs. They may have held positions not only at the head office but at a plant. However, since the number of English-speaking executives in the company is limited, the executives who deal with foreign businessmen, such as international operations or export department managers, may have remained in the same position for years.

The visiting executive should be careful not to be misled by the "managerial" title which the Japanese executive holds. It is said that there are so many managers in one large Japanese company that if you wad up a sheet of paper and toss it into the room blind, it will surely hit a "manager." This is partly because the average age of Japanese employees at the larger companies is getting higher and promotions (or more accurately salaries) are determined by seniority. For instance, the average age of employees at the larger trading firms is said to be around 40. In one company, about 60% of the 12,000 employees are said to be officially deputy section manager or better.

Many of these "managers" have no subordinates, nor have they any supervisory responsibility. Instead, they are engaged in staff functions, and the managerial title simply refers to their status and not to any supervisory function.

Thus it is necessary for a foreign visitor to distinguish between "supervisory managers" and "non-supervisory managers," and then to be mindful of the many limitations on even the "supervisory managers" within the organization.

(*May* 1980)

2
Managerial Overtime

● *In a Japanese company, a man is "developed" into a manager.*

Did you hear the one about the Japanese manager in a foreign company who wanted overtime pay for the time he spent playing golf with a customer? One American personnel manager that I told this to grinned and said, "It's amazing that he didn't ask for a hardship allowance, too."

One of the tasks for the foreign company in Japan is to make managers feel they are part of the management team. There is at least one foreign company I know of in Japan where the "managers" who work overtime invariably end up dining at a nearby restaurant and, being unable to charge for overtime, charge dinner to the company account. If they were managers in the real sense of the word, of course, they would not think of charging for overtime even if they worked on holidays. More often than not, however, the title "manager" refers to their position whether the position entails supervisory or managerial responsibilities or not. As a result, these "managers" who are not allowed to manage do not see themselves as part of the management. On the other hand, since the organization chart says they are managers, they do not qualify for overtime pay and end up charging the company for dinner.

In a Japanese company, a man is "developed" into a manager. In the framework of lifetime employment, a long apprenticeship precedes any promotion to a managerial position. Upon joining a company after graduation, he works under the close supervision of his *kacho* to learn the ropes and to learn how to get along with his boss, peers, and, later, subordinates. Many years of learning precede his becoming a manager, and being a manager is therefore a state of mind in which the person feels responsible for his subordinates as well as for his company. Because of his lifetime commitment to the company, even the newcomer has a strong attachment to the company from the very beginning. When he becomes a manager, his loyalty and allegiance to the company are reinforced.

A large Japanese company usually only recruits new graduates in April. The recruiting job is handled by the personnel department, and the new employees are distributed throughout various sections in the company. Mid-career recruiting is rare, and management seldom fires anyone. As a result, the manager cannot select his own subordinates, since personnel assignments are made by the personnel manager working closely with top management. In a way, it might be said that the Japanese manager is not as profit conscious as his Western counterpart because he is not able to deploy the people under his command for maximum effectiveness.

In foreign companies newly established in Japan, a man is appointed and "becomes" a manager without going through such a preparatory period or psychological adjustment.

In a foreign company, a department manager often hires his own people and asks the personnel manager to do the necessary paperwork. As a result, most personnel functions are left with the department manager himself, and the personnel department has a skeleton staff with very little personnel authority. The personnel department is probably the least appreciated department at foreign companies in Japan. By comparison, it is not uncommon for the personnel department at large Japanese companions to have up to 100 employees at the head office alone. Among Japanese companies, one of the personnel manager's most important functions is to serve as a clearing house for information and to smooth over friction among people or departments within the company. He spots the early warning signals and tries to resolve the situation before it becomes an overt issue in the company. He often acts as troubleshooter and ambassador of friendship without portfolio from department to department. Where the personnel department is doing its job with a mere skeleton staff, the personnel manager may not be able to adequately perform his unofficial duties as troubleshooter and/or communicator.

Where a majority of the employees have joined the company in mid-career, and not immediately after graduation as is the case in most Japanese companies, the employees are unlikely to have the same "Japanese" outlook towards the company. The same obviously holds true for managers as well.

First, there is less loyalty and allegiance to the company. Second, employees tend to be independent-minded and less dependent on their colleagues in the company, thus minimizing the flow of communication both horizontally and vertically. Since top-management positions are often reserved for expatriate managers, Japanese managers tend to feel "victimized," which is another reason why they do not identify themselves as managers in spite of their managerial titles.

Being a manager in Japan is a state of mind combining both mental processes and identification with the company.

Where either is lacking, the man may have a managerial title but will not be doing a manager's job.

Employee training and development has a special place in Japanese companies. Since employees are going to work for the company all their lives, top management is concerned with developing the employees at all levels. As such, Japanese companies offer an almost inexhaustible range of employee programs.

The Isetan department store is typical. In April 1976 alone, Isetan sponsored a total of ten different employee seminars on such subjects as company merchandising policy, introductory floor sales techniques, orientation programs for newly-hired employees, point of purchase (POP) lettering techniques, and what the customer expects at POP. In addition, "cultural" subjects such as horseback riding, painting, the kimono graces, and baking, as well as various sporting events were available.

When there is such a constant flow of information and personalized contact between management and employees, even the dissatisfied employees have no time to feel victimized.

(February 1978)

3
The Pitfall of Brilliance

*●Sometimes it's better if the expatriate manager
doesn't understand Japanese business practices.*

Does an expatriate manager have to be smart in order to
be successful in Japan? Not really, says a friend of mine who
has long been associated with foreign companies in Japan.
In fact, he says, the expatriate manager who has had an
impeccable record of success in his previous positions in the
U.S. or Europe is more likely to fail in Japan.

Needless to say, there are some fundamental ingredients
that make for successful business anywhere in the world.
Therefore, it is quite natural for a manager who was successful
in the U.S. or Europe to try to repeat the same magic formula
of success in Japan.

However, the Japanese business environment is different,
and the rules of the games are miles apart and are often in-
compatible. Therefore, the more successful he has been elsewhere in the world, the more difficult it is for him to make
the necessary adjustments for success in Japan. The proud
manager may be obsessed with the formula that worked in
other parts of the world and consequently reluctant to accept
the realities of business in Japan.

According to my friend, "Expatriates generally cannot and
do not understand these unique Japanese practices. Further,
they do not wish to understand them. Even if they do under-

stand these practices, they cannot believe them. And, finally, I don't think they should try to understand these Japanese practices. Because even if they do understand them, they are too set in their ways to change anyway."

This friend of mine is by no means a chauvinist. On the contrary, he is a mature, well-informed businessman whose judgement I value. Therefore, his remark struck me like a thunderbolt since it seemed as if he were repeating that familiar litany, "East is East and West is West, and never the twain shall meet." It also sounded as if he were adamantly opposed to standard international business cliches of mutual understanding, intercultural communication, and getting to know each other better.

There are many management practices that have been noted as typically Japanese, including lifetime employment, seniority-based wages, collective decision making, the predominantly "enterprise" union labor movement, and the complicated marketing and distribution channels, to name just a few.

When a proud and successful manager arrives in Japan for the first time and is confronted with these unique Japanese management practices, his first reaction is to dismiss them as wrong-headed. He feels that there is something wrong with the system and that the system should therefore be changed. Instead of seeking ways to work within Japan's complex distribution channels, for example, he condemns them as another invisible trade barrier and tries to apply the same magic formula which worked elsewhere. This is probably why my friend said that expatriates do not wish to understand unique Japanese practices.

A Japanese sales manager once told me that he still does not really understand consumer trade practices even after having been in the business for some 20 years. He cited the example of one retailer who does a fine job of selling since he likes the wholesaler he deals with: the wholesaler talked to him at a party. He said that he still finds it difficult to understand the rebate and kick-back system.

Japan has developed such complicated systems in all walks of life in part because of the high value placed on personal contacts. As a result of this personalization, most decisions are situation-oriented. In other words, one must "be there" and be physically and psychologically involved in order to really understand what is going on, whether the subject is marketing, sales, personnel, or labor. Accordingly, the expatriate manager who thinks he understands Japanese practices may be at a critical point in his career, and this is probably what my friend meant when he said that expatriates should not try to understand Japanese practices.

A Japanese proverb says that a superficial understanding of military tactics is likely to cause casualties. This is perhaps akin to the Western saying that a little learning is a dangerous thing.

From the standpoint of the expatriate, it is always safest to assume that he does not understand Japanese management practices and should therefore rely on his Japanese subordinates' judgment as much as possible. A successful manager may do better if he starts his first day in Japan by "unlearning" his successful experiences of the past. Japanese managers complain that their expatriate managers and head-office personnel often tell them what to do but seldom ask why something is done the way it is in Japan. Ask us why more often, they insist, but leave it to us to work out the plan of action.

This said, however, there are several musts for long-term success in Japan. The first and foremost, and yet the least understood, is to foster employee confidence in the company. If they feel that the company is reliable and is going to look after their interests, and that their own future is at one with the company's future, they will give the company their unconditional loyalty and support. There is no better way to motivate Japanese employees than to instill a sense of security. Without this sense of security, without this confidence that the company is looking after them, the first thing employees will do after they get to the office in the morning is to pick up the paper and read the want-ads.

For employees, security is manifested in various ways: when a manager starts hiring and firing at will, nobody is going to stake his future on the company. Under the circumstances, it will become increasingly difficult for the management to hire qualified personnel, and the better-caliber personnel will not stay long in the company either.

Security also means well-organized personnel practices. The employees must know that the company's salary practices are fair. However, in many foreign companies in Japan where mid-career recruiting is the rule, individual salary schedules are decided through personal negotiations. In the process, due consideration is not always given to the existing pay levels, and this frequently results in an unbalanced and demoralizing pay schedule.

So perhaps I should qualify my friend's answer. You do not have to be brilliant to be successful in Japan, but you do have to be smart enough to know what you do not know.

(*April* 1978)

4

The Corked Bottle

● *We want others to infer what we meant from*
what we did not say.

On January 14, 1978, just as I was about to putt for par
on the 18th hole at the Ohito Country Club, the green started
to roll up and down like an ocean wave. Needless to say, I
missed the putt. Of course, I have been known to miss 30-foot
putts even without earthquakes, but it is a convenient lead-in
for this month's essay.

Japan is a country beset with earthquakes and volcanic
explosions. The pent-up subterranean energy gradually builds
up until one day it explodes. Similarly, there may be something explosive about the Japanese, at least from the outsider's
point of view, since we tend to bottle our frustrations up
inside us instead of venting them little by little.

Take, for instance, the recent incident of two junior high
school students who killed some of their classmates. These
two had been constantly teased by the more aggressive young-
sters in the class, and they resorted to a rather extreme measure to put an end to their plight. Afterwards, their parents,
teachers, and neighbors were quoted as saying, "It is incredible. These boys are usually so quiet and well-behaved." Yet
it may be precisely because they had been so quiet and well-
behaved that their resentment built up until it exploded in
this extreme and violent outlet.

One outstanding difference between Japanese and Western TV dramas and movies is the lack of confrontation among Japanese actors. In a typical American drama, a couple who are deeply in love with each other may be talking happily one moment and arguing violently the next. This would almost never happen in a Japanese drama. The heroine may be deeply hurt in the course of the conversation, but her expression will be much subdued. However, this does not mean that the Japanese heroine is any less hurt. It simply means that she swallows her anger and tries to dissipate it inside her. Yet the chances are that a person's feelings will find some expression even if it is not verbal. I recall the story of a Japanese woman who accepted the news of her husband's death with calm and grace outwardly, but it was later found that she had torn the handkerchief which she held underneath the table. I believe that frustrations often build up in Japan because the Japanese do not place so much value and trust in verbal communication. A famous *haiku* by Basho reads:

Mono-ieba	When we utter words
Kuchibiru samushi	Our lips feel chilly.
Aki-no-kaze	Autumn winds.

This *haiku* describes the helpless feeling that we often encounter in trying to communicate verbally. Rather than placing our trust in verbal communication, we often want others to infer what we want to say from what we did not say and from our mannerisms.

Sometimes when my children are out and I am at home watching TV or having tea with just my wife, I say, "How happy I am!" However, this outward expression of contentment only makes my wife angry, since she knows I often facetiously remark on my contentment when I am bored.

My own experience when I first went to the U.S. some 20 years ago is also relevant here. I was staying at a hotel in downtown Chicago and caught a cold. Feeling, and doubtless looking, very ill, I was picking at my breakfast at the cafeteria in the hotel and, the typical Japanese, hoping someone would notice that I was ill and offer to help. People glanced at me, but no one came to my rescue. At the time, I thought that Americans were a very cold and indifferent people. It was only later that I was told I should have asked for help and the other people would have been only too happy to help me. But novice that I was, I assumed that the Americans would understand my plight telepathically. After all, I was sending all the right messages in Japanese.

Expatriate managers in Japan often fail to notice these distress signals from their employees. For instance, there may be a very capable man in the company whose contribution is dearly appreciated and who is known to be getting paid less than he is worth. But the man has never asked for a raise, and the manager thinks that he is happy with his current salary. On the other hand, the man feels that he has been working so hard and making such a contribution to the company that the company should acknowledge this by paying him more. For years, the man may go along dissatisfied with his pay and disappointed that his boss does not take steps to get him a raise. He feels it is his boss's fault for not having done anything about it. When the man finally musters up his courage to come to his boss and ask for a pay raise, the chances are that he is quite emotionally overwrought.

That is also why unions are born overnight, almost out of the blue, in foreign companies. Employee dissatisfactions may have been there for a long time, but unless management notices the distress signals and communicates properly with its employees, the only thing left is the explosion of pent-up forces which erupt in a bitter emotional confrontation.

Japanese management is usually mindful of two aspects in the field of personnel administration: one is to encourage the constant flow of information and communication between management and employees as well as among employees, and the other is to encourage and strengthen the sense of participation and comradeship among employees. I suspect that many in-house seminars and meetings held at Japanese companies exist for no other purpose than to strengthen the sense of belonging and to identify employees' aspirations and grievances. Management should not wait for the employees to come to them. Instead, management should provide opportunities for employees to speak out, and should even try to guess what is on their employees' minds.

(*March* 1978)

5

The Continuity Premium

● *Every company has its one-man broadcasting station.*

In an earlier article, I wrote that gaining employee confidence in the company is one of the most important prerequisites for long-term success in Japan and that such confidence must be based upon the sense of security which management instills in employees. At its worst, security means the status quo ad infinitum. Yet at its best, it can cushion change, and therefore even enhance evolution.

People everywhere hate to see the status quo disrupted, since this implies disorder, uncertainty, and insecurity. Japanese management is thus exceptionally cautious in introducing changes, since they are afraid that the prospect of change may unduly alarm their employees. This is particularly true in implementing policy and organizational changes. A skillful manager usually has informal communication channels within the company and among his subordinates. There are usually some key employees or union members in the company who serve as a "private broadcasting station." First, an informal message is broadcast on a trial basis and the feedback obtained. By the time the final message is relayed to all employees through normal channels, chances are that they are all aware of the new development and at least psychologically prepared for it. No Japanese manager would be so naive as to forgo this ritual before announcing a major decision.

These Japanese behind-the-scenes preparations are sometimes called *nemawashi*, which is gardener's jargon. Literally, *nemawashi* means to bind the roots of a tree before transplanting it. When the tree to be transplanted is chosen, the gardener first digs around it, cutting off the smaller roots in the ground and trimming the branches to maintain a balance between roots and branches. Later, the tree is dug out and the clump of dirt containing the roots wrapped in a straw mat. The uprooted tree is then laid on the ground for a few days in order to let it rest up for the coming trip. Only afterwards is the tree removed and transplanted in a new location.

In transplanting a new idea, such as organizational changes or personnel reassignments, the Japanese executive is no less assidious about this *nemawashi* than is the gardener transplanting a valuable tree.

In a country like Japan, where some companies have been in business several hundred years, long-standing relations between firms are great assets in themselves. Banks often consider the length of the association with a particular company in assessing the company's credit-worthiness. The longer the association, the deeper the mutual trust and understanding between firms is assumed to be.

Little wonder, then, that the Japanese company wishes to establish a long-lasting relationship with its suppliers, distributors, and customers. At times, one side may even accept a temporary loss so as not to hurt their long-standing relations. When this occurs, there is an expectation on the part of the company which took the loss that it will be offset by a particularly lucrative business transaction later. Such expectations are only possible when both parties have been doing business for years and can safely assume that their relationship will continue for many more years to come. As a result of this immediate fluidity based upon long-range stability, it is often difficult to define the business terms between the manufacturer and the wholesaler except as a "give-and-take" relation.

However, it may be difficult for the expatriate manager to be so philosophical about such temporary losses in long-standing business relationships when the head office is judging his performance by the quarterly, monthly, or even weekly bottom line. Indeed, this Japanese "penny-foolish and pound-wise" indulgence of other people's circumstances may even appear insane or at best unrealistic to the expatriate manager.

Very often the first reaction by the head office in New York, when they are dissatisfied with the job their Japanese subsidiary's wholesaler is doing, is to get rid of them and find another one. Hearing that the wholesaler gets a 35% commision, the head office asks if the wholesaler has warehouse facilities. The answer is no. Then the head office asks if perhaps the wholesaler provides the field sales force. Again, the answer is no. The order which naturally follows is to get rid of them. However, this may be the only wholesaler the company can deal with in Japan, and there may be no other alternative.

While a Western expatriate's performance is checked quarterly, and there is thus a great incentive to improve the *current* profitability, the immediate pressures on the Japanese executive appear to be much less. In the first place, the chief executive officer in a Japanese company has been chosen from within the company, and the stockholders meeting has only a perfunctory role. Most board members are also officers in the company, and they seldom look over the president's shoulder at operating decisions they have helped make. The major decisions are made at executive meetings presided over by the president. Nor, given the framework of lifetime employment, are the other department managers subject to immediate demotion or dismissal for a poor showing.

Thus Japanese executives can afford to think of corporate interests in a longer time span than their Western counterparts, and Western expatriates, conditioned to expect swift justice for every success or failure, often find it difficult to adjust to the Japanese style of corporate relations conceived on such a long-term basis.

(*May* 1978)

6

The Saber vs. the Revolver

● *Just a rattle is enough to get the job done.*

An American company recently waged a campaign to recruit promising students from leading Japanese universities by offering summer work to seniors from such prestigious universities as the University of Tokyo and Hitotsubashi University and offering post-graduation jobs to the ones who had shown the most potential over the summer. In selecting the best several students, they evaluated everybody's on-the-job performance very carefully, being careful not to place an undue emphasis on English capability and to base their evaluation on job performance, leadership, organizational adaptability, and personality. This was a well-known American company with a worldwide reputation, and the recruiter was confident that the students would gladly accept the offer. Not only did the company offer a starting salary twice the amount the students could reasonably expect to receive at a better-known Japanese company, there were also good prospects for being sent overseas.

The recruiter was thus quite shocked when every last student turned him down. He later found that these students joined such companies as Fuji Bank, Mitsubishi Corporation, Toyota Motor Co., Ltd., Hitachi, Ltd., and MITI.

This episode is illustrative of the fact that the criteria for selecting qualified graduates are probably the same for Japanese and American companies. It also demonstrates the difficulty a foreign company has hiring top-notch students in Japan.

Foreign companies doing business in and with Japan are often said to face a number of invisible trade barriers, not the least of which is the difficulty of attracting enough qualified personnel.

One of the biggest concerns for graduating Japanese students selecting a job is "security." They want to work in a company which offers lifetime security along with the prospect of ever-increasing responsibilities. The large and well-established Japanese companies listed on the first section of the Tokyo Stock Exchange employ students from only a few "designated" universities. These "designated" universities usually include the national universities and a few high-ranking private universities. Students from non-designated universities are not even interviewed. Therefore, it is essential that a student get into a leading university if he wants to work for a leading company. This is why there is such keen competition for admission to the leading universities. Those "elite" students who took summer jobs at the American company probably already had their career plans at leading Japanese companies or in government service mapped out by that time.

Right or wrong, there is a widespread stigma attached to working for a foreign company doing business in Japan because it is assumed that the job security is low and that a person may be fired at the head-office's whim whenever something goes wrong or the bottom line looks bad. The prospects for promotion may be much greater in a foreign company, the starting salaries may be much better, and there may be a greater opportunity for overseas assignments, but there is still this overriding fear of job insecurity.

In Japan, every president has a saber in his hand and nobody else is allowed to hold the saber; while in the U.S., every manager at every level has a revolver on his hip. But the Japanese president does not use the saber to stab his subordinates. All he needs to do is to rattle it. Just a rattle is enough for him to get the job done and to control the resources at his command.

In Japan, it is customary for a manager elected to the board to resign from the company before accepting his new post. Since he has become an employer and is thus no longer an employee, he submits an official letter of resignation, receives his severance pay, and is then rehired to serve on the board.

In some large companies, the president is reported to ask all new board members to also submit letter of resignation from the board, this one with the date blank. If and when the president wants a board member to retire, all he has to do is to fill in the date. This is the extent of the power held by the president in Japan. However, he seldom fills in the dates in such letters, and it is probably this restraint that gives him such unchallenged authority in the company.

On the other hand, in the typical American company, just as in the western movie, every manager wears a six-shooter strapped to his hip, and he not only draws his gun but even fires at other people in the same company.

There is no doubt but that the graduating Japanese student prefers the distant rattle of the saber to the constant threat of the revolver at his head, no matter how great the possible rewards may be for winning in the latter situation.

There was a time when being assigned to an overseas post spelled success and was the shortest path to advancement and promotion for people working for Japanese companies. However, as the scope of Japanese business has become more international and more overseas posts have been created both in the major metropolitan centers and in the developing countries, the lure of overseas posts has faded and there is an increasing tendency for Japanese businessmen to prefer to stay in Japan.

The children of these expatriate Japanese executives usually have a hard time adjusting to the Japanese school system after they come back, and they are greatly handicapped in preparing for the university entrance examinations. Rather than disadvantage their children, the parents are often forced to leave the children in Japan. Sometimes the husband has to leave his entire family in Japan and go overseas by himself.

The Japanese manager stationed overseas regards his position with mixed feelings. On one hand, he has the advantage of special visibility to top management; and on the few occasions when the top management visits his country, he can work closely with them and attend to their needs. Most of the time, however, he has the feeling of being isolated thousands of miles away from the home office and not knowing what is going on there. Sometimes, the time away from the head office means lost opportunities, since he loses valuable contacts which may be important for his later career. These are some of the reasons why overseas assignments have lost their lure for Japanese executives.

People who join the company immediately upon graduation have decided to make the company their careers, and management can count on their untiring dedication and commitment. This is why most Japanese companies place such emphasis on recruiting new graduates each year.

However, unless the company has over 1,000 employees and unless it has a dozen people in its personnel department doing recruiting alone, it will likely find it difficult to start a regular program of recruiting new graduates each year.

Since most foreign companies in Japan are medium-sized in terms of number of employees, they are handicapped by the invisible trade barrier of not being able to attract many top-notch students.

Consequently, most of them are forced to turn to mid-career recruiting programs under which most people join the company with a different set of expectations and values. Most personnel problems that occur in foreign companies may be traced to the fact that they are handicapped in recruiting new graduates out of college.

(September 1978)

7

In the Long Walk

●*Life is like walking a long way carrying a heavy load.*

Ieyasu Tokugawa, the man who laid the foundations for 250 years of rule by the Tokugawa Shogunate, once said,

A man's life
is like walking a long way
carrying a heavy load.
It is not wise to hurry too much.
He who regards inconvenience as the norm
has no cause for complaint,

and he who desires overmuch
should recall when he had naught.
Consider patience the foundation of enduring peace
and anger thy enemy.
He who knows only how to prevail
and not how to yield
puts himself in peril.
Blame thyself,
but never others.
Falling a little short
is better than going to excess.

Ieyasu was a shrewd *samurai* who was noted for his patience and perseverance.

Now, centuries later, Ieyasu remains quite popular and much quoted among Japanese business leaders. I suspect that this popularity rests largely upon his far-sighted strategy in building a dynasty which lasted for over 250 years. Even today, it appears that people assuming top management positions in Japan need these same qualities of a firm and long-term "vision" for the company plus patience and cautiousness in its implementation.

When there is a change in the top management position in the West, the new man is expected to bring in a new strategy which is different in style or substance from his predecessors. In fact, this difference is often the reason he has been hired by the company in the first place.

When a new president is appointed in Japan, on the other hand, he is very likely to say, "I am afraid I am not ready to assume this important position yet, but I will do my best, studying what my predecessor has done and faithfully following in his footsteps."

It is said that when a new manager is appointed in Japan, he does nothing in the new post for the first six months; this so that he can thoroughly familiarize himself with what is going on. Recently, a former high-ranking government official joined the top management of a large steel firm. But before assuming his duties as president, he toured the field offices and plants, visiting with employees and customers alike for several months. All of this was necessary to establish himself.

Whether it is a top- or middle-management position, a position in the government, or whatever, the person who has been given a new post of importance usually tries to pursue the same policy line as his predecessor and does not expect to change anything overnight.

Just as in the feudal days of Ieyasu, employees in modern Japan work for their employer for life. Theirs is a lifetime commitment to the company. As a result, regardless of who may be appointed president, he has the same key personnel in the company reporting to him. In the West, a new president who is brought into an organization has the freedom to choose his own team, even bringing them from outside if necessary, to implement his new policies.

Changes in strategy are impossible unless the people concerned thoroughly understand the implications of the changes and modify their behavior accordingly. The quickest way to do this is to bring in a new management team used to the new concepts. For instance, when a company wants to introduce a new marketing strategy, the fastest and easiest way will be to reshuffle the staff and stack the marketing staff with people familiar with the new marketing concept. However, such a course is difficult to pursue under Japan's system of lifelong employment. Therefore, even when Japanese top management recognizes the need for change, they do not expect to make it overnight.

Like Ieyasu Tokugawa, they have found that the "don't hurry" philosophy works in Japan. Instead of forcing changes from above, they are content to wait until a consensus forms from below.

Most Western managers are less patient and less tolerant of resistance to change. I have even seen cases where expatriate managers aroused considerable customer resentment by abruptly announcing overnight changes in their marketing policies. While Japanese managers consider changes over a timespan of several years, most Western managers are eager to institute complete changes within months, weeks, and even days.

Given the lifelong employment system in Japan, one of management's prime responsibilities is to instill feelings of employee confidence and trust towards the management. This most often entails practicing a policy of continuity. When management fails to do this and changes policies too often, employees will soon begin to wonder whether management really cares about them, and if they really want to spend the rest of their working lives with a flighty company like this.

I recently had occasion to talk with a foodstuff salesman whose boss constantly reviewed his performance. When he found out that his monthly salary was ¥20 (about 10¢) less than his peers', he immediately suspected that he had gotten a lower rating than the other people. He was greatly distressed at this and fretted about it so much that he finally went to his boss to ask for an explanation. To an outsider, ¥20 a month may not seem like much. Objectively, it is not. However, it mattered a great deal to him. In the first place, if he keeps getting ¥20 less every month, it means that the management regards him as less valuable than his peers. If this continues for several years, he may even be passed over when his peers are to be promoted to managerial ranks. Even if he is promoted, it may be a year or two late. This is when it makes a big difference in terms of income, since a manager receives a host of fringe benefits and allowances that, on an annual basis, could easily make a difference of ¥1–2 million between the manager and the non-manager.

Thus, when the young salesman took issue with his boss, he was arguing not about the ¥20 difference in salary but about his own entire future with the company. Everything management does has a way of affecting the long-term prospects of every employee.

Most foreign companies doing business in Japan are now going through the soul-searching stage of "Japanizing" their management. This involves overhauling their personnel system and thoroughly reviewing their compensation schedules and hiring practices.

It also involves studies to see if the management system is geared to long-term success in Japan. In all of this, they should never lose sight of the long-term perspective from which Japanese employees view management.

(September 1979)

8

Focusing on Japan

●Japanese firms request such extensive data as to make one wonder whether they plan to buy the product or make it themselves.

Nordson K.K., a manufacturer of adhesive application equipment and coating and sealing application equipment in Japan, had a 1978 per-capita income good enough to rank them 384th among the top 50,000 Japanese companies according to *Nikkei Business* magazine.

According to Toshiro Akasaki, president of Nordson K.K. and Doboy K.K. (a division of Nordson Corporation), the parent company's perception of the Japanese market has been the decisive factor in Nordson's success in Japan. The U.S. Nordson Corporation regards the Pacific market as most crucial, and expects total sales in the Pacific region to surpass U.S. sales in 10 years. Needless to say, Japan is the single most important market in the Pacific. With this awareness of the Japanese market's importance, the head office devotes extra care, attention, and assistance to the management of its subsidiary in Japan.

Akasaki is also vice president of the Nordson parent company, which enables him to maintain direct contact with the president of the parent corporation as well as with all the other vice presidents at the head office. He visits the head office in Amherst, Ohio, several times a year, and it is relatively easy for him to get the top management to understand what is going on in Japan.

Accordingly, the employees of the Japanese subsidiary are able to correspond freely with their opposite numbers in Amherst, and there are frequent visits back and forth. When non-English-speaking engineers are sent to the head office for technical consultations, an interpreter is provided to facilitate the smooth transfer of technology. Constant exchanges of information with U.S. and European distributors are also encouraged, and a special budget is maintained for that purpose. Extra effort is made to produce products meeting the Japanese specifications and requirements. There is a recognition that Japan is the most difficult and competitive market in the world, and that anyone who is successful in Japan can be successful anywhere.

Japanese customers are noted for requesting detailed product specifications and test data. Whereas a modicum of practical data on the product's use is sufficient in the U.S. and Europe, Japanese customers are not satisfied unless they receive almost incredibly detailed data. Indeed Japanese customers sometimes request such extensive data on the product as to make one wonder whether they intend to buy it or to make it themselves.

The Japanese customers are probably just as fussy about after-care service. Therefore, Nordson places particular emphasis on maintaining a proper stock of spare parts at all times and providing full maintenance service. In fact, Nordson has just as many service engineers as it does sales engineers.

Sometimes the Japanese customer makes what appears to be an unreasonable request. For instance, in coating a packing case, the Japanese customer often requests that the spraying equipment should be able to coat not only the outside of the case but also the inside, which means a special and extra alteration of the equipment. Japan is probably the only country in the world where the customer is concerned about coating the inside of a case, which nobody else would see anyway. Nevertheless, Nordson does its best to accommodate such requests.

Akasaki believes that, in order to be successful in Japan, the parent corporation should be willing to wait for at least three years before evaluating a particular business decision. The Western manager tries to evaluate corporate performance on much too short a basis, such as the quarterly report or immediate return on investment. In Nordson's case, they want to make sure that they do not lose sight of the longer-term prospects for the company three, five, and even ten years in the future. Accordingly, Akasaki has not had to worry too much about the short-term ups and downs, and has been able to delegate most operational decisions to his subordinates while he thinks about the company's future in Japan.

As long as the long-term plan is on target, management is prepared to accept temporary declines in business, since some long-term gains may have to be made at the expense of short-term profits.

It appears that there are a good number of foreign companies in Japan which are doing just the opposite of what Nordson has been doing. To many, Japan is just another market where extra products are dumped, and there is no conscious effort made to comply with local requirements.

As long as the market remains of peripheral concern, there is no doubt that their business in Japan will remain limited, and most of their local employees' time will be spent apologizing for delivery delays, parts shortages, and faulty order processing. Under the circumstances, it becomes increasingly difficult for them to have any pride in their product or company.

Little wonder that the employee turnover remains high, sometimes as much as 40%.

The president or general manager of a foreign subsidiary in Japan, whether he be an expatriate or a Japanese, is often the only person who has a direct line of communication with the parent company, and other middle-management people are often discouraged from communicating with their opposite numbers in the parent corporation. When this is the case, the workload is centered at the top and there is little delegation of authority to subordinates. As a result, the organization soon loses its esprit de corps and lapses into incompetence.

When the middle-management people are constantly told what to do and there is little room for them to exercise independent initiative, they soon become followers unable or unwilling to make that extra effort for self-development. Such a company is on its deathbed.

One manager summed up the predicament of his company in Japan succinctly by saying, "The product is OK. The market is OK. But the management is no good."

(*October* 1979)

9
Taking It to the Top

●*Writing a letter addressed to "Mr. President" is the surest way not to contact the top management.*

Foreign businessmen wishing to deal directly with the top management of a well-established Japanese company often complain that it is difficult to discover the protocol for visiting them.

Most large Japanese companies have someone whose main responsibility is to assist the top management in international business. He has the authority to review and sort out incoming mail, to follow up on that mail which needs special attention, and to route mail to the top for a decision. At the same time he is able to reroute mail to other departments even if it is addressed to the president. He often accompanies senior executives on their overseas trips. He is not old enough to be a member of the board. However, since he has the confidence of the top management, he may be one of the most influential executives in the company.

This person may carry a title such as general manager of the president's office, senior coordinator, manager of the executive office, or even special executive assistant. Likewise, he may be in the general affairs department, overseas department, or the export department. But no matter what his title, all correspondence from overseas usually passes over his desk for review.

A foreign executive who deals with the top management eventually finds out who this person is in the company. But eventually is not soon enough for an executive who is going to deal with a Japanese company, and he is well advised to find out who that person is first.

In this connection, it should be borne in mind that the typical Japanese company does not have anyone like the Western executive secretary. In most Western companies, the executive secretary assigned to top management is in charge of such matters as handling incoming mail and phone calls, making appointments, filing, and, of course, letter writing. From the standpoint of the Western executive, the simplest way to make an appointment is therefore to ask his secretary to call up the other person's secretary and have her make the arrangements. However, the other person does not have a secretary in a Japanese company.

It is true that Japanese companies have a "*hisho-ka*" or secretary's office. This *hisho-ka* is manned by a small staff to deal with such matters as public relations, customer relations, government relations, and stockholder relations, as well as to assist top management affairs, including making appointments with *Japanese* customers. These responsibilities may sometimes be shared with the general affairs department. For international business, however, since special expertise is required, most questions are routed to that special person I spoke of earlier and not to the *hisho-ka*.

Even once you know who is really in charge of arranging appointments for the top management, it is a good idea to remember why these people are there. I recently asked an old classmate of mine who was one of the three official secretaries to a former Prime Minister what his most important job was.

He said, "Very simply, my job was to sort out requests for appointments with the Prime Minister and to turn them down." People in the *hisho-ka* and people handling international appointments for top management no doubt feel the same way. They are usually engaged in confidential work, and it is the most prudent, cautious, and secretive people who are selected for this work.

A friend of mine who holds such a position suggests that writing a letter addressed to "Mr. President" is the surest way *not* to contact the top management of a Japanese company for the first time, since the letter will most likely get lost in the shuffle from desk to desk. He also suggests staying away from the *hisho-ka*.

He told me of a successful ploy employed by a European company. Urgently needing to talk on the phone directly with the president, they telexed him first to explain what they wanted to discuss and asked if it would be possible to talk with the Japanese president on the phone. When the answer was affirmative, a time was set for the phone call. When the international call came through, my friend was there to interpret for the president and the issue was successfully settled.

A telex or international telephone call direct to the president is often effective, since it demands an answer and is imposing enough to clamor for attention. By the same token, international telephone calls are often used by international executive recruiting firms contacting qualified candidates for placement in multinational positions, since an overseas call direct to the candidate's home is both "exciting" and conducive to a decision.

In the West, it is quite common for the secretary to initiate the call and to transfer the line to her boss when the other person is on the line. In Japan, this would be regarded as impolite. Since a Japanese executive is not accustomed to using a secretary, he feels somewhat put out when he picks up the phone and finds himself put on hold by some woman.

When a local representative is used to confirm an appointment on a very important issue, it is advised that he call on the man in charge in person rather than on the telephone.

A friend who works at a company which manufactures and markets industrial machinery worldwide tells me that there is a daily flood of visitors and letters demanding immediate attention. There are brochures from government agencies and local municipalities all over the world offering incentives to induce the company to establish local manufacturing plants. And there are letters from distributors and wholesalers from all over the world interested in handling the company's products.

There are requests for contributions from universities and charitable bodies. Interviews with reporters have to be arranged. In November last year alone, his company received 45 different overseas groups totaling 350 people who wished to visit the company and study its plant operations.

It should be noted also that internationalization has progressed to the point where the top management is often out of Japan, and this also makes it increasingly difficult to arrange a personal appointment in Japan.

On being shown into the special room reserved for meetings with the top management, the visitor will usually find some paintings hung on the walls and a few other art pieces displayed in the room. Traditionally, etiquette demands that the caller not sit down but spend the time until his host comes in looking at these art objects, almost as if he were in a museum, and some comment of appreciation is a very acceptable icebreaker.

(*January* 1980)

10
Different Culture, Different Problems

● *Maintaining a low turnover is just as much*
an end as it is a means in Japan.

Susumu Morikawa, senior general manager for the Musical
Movements Division of Sankyo Seiki, reports that many
Japanese and Western managers visited him while he was
managing director of Sankyo Seiki (Malaysia). Whereas the
Japanese executives usually asked him what the worker turnover ratio was and commiserated with him when he said that it
was over 30%, Western executives rarely brought up the issue
of worker turnover, since they took it for granted that a high
turnover ratio is a fact of life which management has to live
with.

After many overseas assignments, Morikawa has come to
realize that a frame of reference entirely different from the
Japanese system must be used in managing people of different
cultural backgrounds. For instance, one of the first things
which management had to do in Malaysia, with its diverse
ethnic mix, was to standardize work procedures. However,
when he tried to introduce the Japanese version of "standardization" into his plant operations in Malaysia, it was very
obvious very soon that it was not going to work.

With Japan's system of lifelong employment, workers have
been working with the same company for years and have

accumulated on-the-job skills. Within the small group that makes up the production unit in the plant, skilled workers tend to go beyond the call of duty and to assist the junior, and hence less-experienced, workers. In helping, the senior worker may even end up doing his subordinate's job from time to time. Efforts for introducing standardization and quality control are thus built around the production unit in the Japanese plant.

Therefore, when measures such as standardization and quality control are introduced to improve productivity, the target is geared to those group members who are the most skilled. Setting such demanding targets also has a way of encouraging workers, enhancing their feelings of solidarity and raising their morale. Sometimes the workers even try to outdo the manual and create their own, even-higher, standards.

On the other hand, this Japanese system does not work where each job is defined by a job description and where an assignment of new duties is understood only in terms of its wage implications. The target for improving productivity must thus be geared to the group's least-skilled members since one cannot expect the senior workers to willingly do their juniors' work. There is more emphasis on the individual's work procedure and not on the procedures for the group as a whole.

In countries where the labor turnover is high, and where the supervisor cannot be expected to spend valuable time training people who will not be there tomorrow, it is imperative that the management have a well-developed, comprehensive training program for individual workers. Likewise, since each individual job is clearly defined, management can provide such training programs to new employees without much difficulty whenever vacancies occur.

On the other hand, when a vacancy occurs in Japan, the

ambiguity of the new worker's role and his dependence on more-skilled workers in the group make it difficult to provide a specific training program for him.

Therefore, in the Japanese context, rapid turnover means the loss of vital skills which integrated and cemented the unit, and poses the difficulty of having to train new workers. Rapid turnover is also synonymous with low morale, lack of cooperative spirit among workers, and difficulty in introducing changes. No wonder that most Japanese executives regard rapid labor turnover as a nightmare.

Maintaining a low labor turnover is thus often just as much an end as it is a means to profitable and stable business in Japan. In some countries, however, where mobility is a way of life, management must be mindful of the balance between a low turnover and the cost of maintaining this low turnover, and must devise some system which works in spite of high labor mobility.

There are even times when a high turnover can be to management's advantage, particularly when it wishes to effect strategic changes. As Morikawa puts it, the Japanese management system is better suited to improving current production methods while the Western management system based on rapid mobility is better suited to innovation.

In dealing with personnel problems for foreign companies doing business in Japan, I have often been asked by Western executives what the single most important concept is in Japanese personnel management. My answer has always been the same: "Give your employees the feeling that management can be trusted and that the company is worthy of employees' investing their lives in it. In short, a feeling of security and a sense of belonging are all-important."

A simple statement? It certainly looks simple. Yet practicing this philosophy will require immense efforts in a host of areas.

First of all, management should start with a systematic recruiting program—hopefully with new graduates. Needless to say, management offering lifelong employment should be careful to select only the best-qualified employees. In order to do this, management is required to develop recruiting expertise, including contacts with leading universities, vocational institutions, and high schools.

Second, management should develop an explicit personnel policy—spelling out where it wishes to go, how it wishes to get there, and how it wishes to treat its employees. This presupposes the existence of a well-organized system and procedures of personnel administration, such as rules of employment, compensation schedules, fringe benefits, and employee development programs. And this further presupposes that management places great importance on personnel functions and is often directly involved in implementing personnel policies.

Third, management should try to develop policies in Japan on the long-term basis. Abrupt policy changes and the lack of long-term perspective are the surest ways to lose employee support, to chill employee enthusiasm, and to make employees wonder whether management really cares about them.

Fourth, efforts should be made to strengthen the feelings of camaraderie and company identification among employees.

The low turnover in Japan is a combination of all these efforts, and in Japan this leads to improved organizational effectiveness.

However, as mentioned earlier, the same frame of reference may not be valid in other parts of the world, and management must always consider the specific country's social and cultural background in formulating an appropriate frame of reference.

(*April* 1980)

PART IV

---

*Management Myopia
or a Bold Approach?*

1

Management Myopia
or a Bold Approach?

● *Japanese executives are often willing to accept temporary losses in the interest of long-term gains.*

In this final chapter, I should like to review some of the outstanding features of Japanese management and, at the risk of oversimplification, to contrast them with the features characterizing Western management.

One of the recurrent themes of Japanese management in the previous chapters has been the concept of continuity and the Japanese preoccupation with long-range implications in decision making.

Put very simply, Japanese executives are always looking to be sure that what they do today will have a positive impact on the company many years from now. Given the framework of permanent employment, they know full well that they will be working for the same company for many years. The same is true of lower-ranking employees as well. It is this future-oriented identification that accounts for their concern with the long-term impact of what they do.

As in any country, it sometimes happens that decisions made from the long-term perspective may entail some sacrifice of short-term profits. When this happens, the "good" Japanese manager is expected to opt for long-term gain. It is taken for granted that building a better future may require current sacrifice.

Employee recruiting is perhaps the prime example. As is well known, Japanese companies usually hire new graduates directly out of school each year. This requires that they make a substantial investment in training and developing these new employees. From the standpoint of assembling a ready work force, it would be better for them to resort to mid-career recruiting. However, Japanese management makes this training investment because they can reap the harvest ten years later when these people have acquired the necessary skills and become the mainstay of the work force.

Similarly, Japanese executives tend to consider their customer relations on a long-term basis. As a result, they often place the priority on developing a long-lasting relationship of sincerity and trust, even if building this relationship requires sustaining a temporary loss.

By the same token, Japanese executives do not get cold feet even if a new product does not show immediate profits. Waiting five years for a particular product to show a profit is not uncommon for the typical Japanese top executive. The reason they do not get panicky is that their performance is not evaluated against the short-term measure of current results. In the framework of lifelong employment, an executive is judged over the total span of his service with the company, and there is thus no need to shine at every moment. Even if the current results are somewhat wanting, he knows that he is not going to be fired for it. Also given the framework of permanent employment, another prime concern for Japanese top management is that of employee welfare.

A typical Japanese equity:debt ratio is 20:80, meaning that the management of a Japanese company is usually more concerned with their bankers than with their stockholders. This is especially true since most Japanese institutional investors refrain from second-guessing unless the company is in serious financial trouble.

Consequently, Japanese management is not under pressure to perform better for the stockholders. Japanese management is not compelled to show ever-better ROI and PER. Since they have long-standing relations with their banks and can turn to the banks rather than the capital market for help, they can more readily make investments of a long-term nature without worrying about the investments' immediate negative impact on the company's current financial position.

This is in sharp contrast to the situation in the U.S., where top management performance is rigorously appraised in terms of annual, quarterly, and even monthly bottom lines. American management is under constant pressure to show improved profits, even at the risk of hurting the company's long-term position.

If the financial return is not high enough, U.S. top management runs the risk of being fired. And of course, the high management turnover makes it all the more difficult to institute long-range programs which will pay off only after the innovator has been fired or moved to another firm.

Japanese-style management does have its drawbacks. For instance, when management is too dependent on borrowings to finance growth, less attention is paid to the sound accumulation of equity capital and management is susceptible to reckless expansion fever.

At the same time, the high overhead structure caused by forward investments and management's virtual inability to lay people off pushes the break-even point for production and sales ever higher. As a result, management must maintain a high operating ratio simply to stay in business. The whole management concept thus evolves around more production, faster expansion, and a bigger market share. Since the loss of even a few percentage points in sales may seriously endanger the company's very ability to survive, this often leads the company into cut-throat price competition.

When management makes a decision for debt-financed, large-scale investment, it runs the risk of catastrophe if the timing is off or the decision is otherwise wrong. On the other hand, when the investment is sound and well justified, aggressive debt-financing of long-term investment, regardless of its possible short-term adverse impact, may turn out to be a major factor in improving a company's competitive edge.

Generally speaking, Japanese management appears to have worked best in industries where (1) high technology was involved, (2) competition was keen, (3) there was a large and expanding market, and (4) scale was an advantage and huge investment was required to enjoy the advantages of size. By the very nature of this definition, the Japanese management style has worked best in international markets in competition with Western companies.

It is also worth noting that this bold approach was often undertaken with the blessings of the government and that there were various institutions which were willing to help, including banks established specifically to provide long-term credit for industries. Another factor which has worked to Japanese management's benefit was that the rapid appreciation of real estate values enabled Japanese companies to borrow heavily by mortgaging real estate. In short, it has been the total system of business and management in Japan which has made this long-term approach possible.

This disparity in styles seems to be at the heart of the differences between Japan and the U.S. in some key industries. The steel industry is a case in point. According to a report by the U.S. Federal Trade Commission, the U.S. steel industry had an $8 advantage over the Japanese industry in major input costs per net ton of steel products in 1956. Yet by 1960, Japan had a cost advantage of $32 per ton. In 1976, the Japanese cost advantage was $120 per ton.

In a report delivered to the Center for International Studies, Harvard University, in April 1980, Associate Professor Kiyoshi Kawahito of Middle Tennessee State University's Business and Economic Research Center identified three reasons why the Japanese steel industry was able to achieve this cost competitiveness: "First, the Japanese industry has swiftly adopted and continuously maintained the world's best technology in steelmaking facilities and in operational practices.

"Secondly, a large Japanese disadvantage before 1960 in the purchase price of two major inputs, coking coal and iron ore, has been mostly eliminated by the opening of new supply sources, and by the drastic decline in ocean freight rates relative to inland freight rates.

"Thirdly, the gap in hourly employment costs between the U.S. and Japanese steel industries has widened over the past twenty-five years.

"This widening has taken place despite a much faster increase in Japanese steel wages. According to FTC data, the hourly labor cost in 1956 was $3.35 in the United States and $0.43 in Japan, with a difference of $2.92. In 1976, the figures became $12.14 and $5.25 respectively, with a gap of $6.89.

"In general, the opposite of the above description of the Japanese steel industry applies to the U.S. steel industry. The industry has made poor investment decisions since the 1950s; it has continually poured funds into rounding-out of old facilities in defiance of changing technological criteria, including scale and location."

There may be many reasons why the U.S. steel industry has made "poor investment decisions" since the 1950s while the Japanese steel industry has been catching up. Yet in hindsight, is it not possible to attribute this at least in part to management's preoccupation with current profitablility and management's reluctance to finance growth when that might endanger the company's current financial position?

If this has taken place in such a vital industry as steel, it is easy to surmise that the same thing has been happening in other key industries such as automobiles, chemicals, home appliances, electronics, and telecommunications.

The financial statement of a typical Japanese company may show such a high debt ratio as to appear close to bankruptcy to many Western managers, but this heavy debt position is buttressed by the strong confidence of those financial institutions which have supported Japanese industry's rapid expansion.

Japanese stockholder attitudes are another factor which has enabled Japanese management to take the long-term approach. While American stockholders are always quick to demand larger dividends, Japanese stockholders have often been content with a much lower level of dividends in the expectation of capital gains made over a longer period of time. As a result, the American system of management yields more stockholder gratification while the Japanese system yields more internationally competitive companies.

Another manifestation of Japanese management's long-term

commitment is in personnel management. What could be more long-term than lifelong employment? Yet in return for this long-term commitment, management receives the workers' wholehearted support, commitment, and dedication to the company.

Employees readily associate and identify with management. Japan has often been referred to as "Japan, Inc." with the implication of close ties between Japanese business and government. But it may be more appropriate to interpret "Japan, Inc." as a company where both management and labor are one and the same. They often share the same values and goals, and they may easily see eye to eye on company policy.

A rapidly growing Japanese company almost invariably has the active participation of workers on such matters as technological innovation, operational methods, quality control, and cost reduction.

Workers at the plant level often form groups to solve particular problems. At Western companies, these problems may be thought to be a management problem and none of the workers' business. As a result, plant problems are left to production engineers or industrial engineers to solve. Not so in Japan.

These Japanese worker groups may go by many names, such as Quality Control circles, "zero-defect" movements, or "no-error" movements. Whatever the name, they are indicative of collective worker participation in creating a workplace compatible with their life goals.

Perhaps the best-known of these groups are the Quality Control circles. QC circles are small groups, usually six or seven workers, who decide on the particular problem to be studied and choose their own leaders for this. By participating in such endeavors collectively, the group's members gain valuable experience in togetherness and fulfilment at the same time as they contribute to better procedures or improved quality control. Their activities are usually conducted during breaks or after work. It is reported that there were over 100,000 "officially recognized" QC circles with the participation of more than one million workers in Japan in 1979.

Nippon Steel Corporation has 8,400 J-K groups involving more than 70% of its 52,000 blue-collar workers. The name "J-K" stands for "Jishu-Kanri," which means self-management. In 1978, these groups successfully attained 15,935 goals and targets, and it is estimated that the J-K activities saved Nippon Steel approximately $5 per ton of steel product in 1978.

Thus it is safe to say that a Japanese company with 50,000 employees has 50,000 profit centers, each of them striving to achieve a better common future by improving productivity and earning bigger profits.

Yutaka Takeda, executive vice president of Nippon Steel, recently told a meeting of the Japan Society in New York how very involved workers are in Nippon Steel's management: "A little over ten years ago, the women who worked on the telephone switchboard at our Nagoya steel works formed a group and began a campaign to reduce the phone bill by at least half. This was their own idea.

"The Nagoya plant is some distance outside the city limits, a fact which accounts for part of its sizable phone bill. At that time, the bill amounted to about ¥8 million a month.

"This campaign was thus aimed at reducing this to no more than ¥4 million. Again let me emphasize the significant point: It was not the section manager in charge who came up with this initiative but these women operators whose primary job consists of saying, 'Hello. One moment please,' and 'Your party is on the line.'

"The women knew that if calls were brief and to the point,

three minutes would be adequate time to complete a piece of business. So they planned a 'shorter-calls campaign' to encourage phone users to keep their calls within three minutes. (The base telephone charge in Japan applies for the first three minutes.)

"They knew, of course, which people in which departments were in the habit of making long calls, and they had the company provide three-minute egg-timers, which were placed on these people's desks with the explanation: 'This is a three-minute timer. Please keep your calls within three minutes.'

"Those who were approached this way apparently resented it at first—after all, their male pride was hurt. But after a while they began to understand the rationale and the movement developed into a team effort which succeeded in reducing the phone bill from ¥8 million to less than ¥4 million."

There is no doubt in my mind that Western executives—particularly top management—are much more competitive and harder working than their Japanese counterparts. On the other hand, they have to work hard at motivating their own unmotivated workers while Japanese workers are just as eager to work for the company as management is.

Japanese top management have been able to pursue a bold long-term approach because there were no short-term demands to check their performance. With the support of the various management, financial, and political systems which favored this approach, they simply did what they thought best for the company in the long run.

In this respect, the gap that appears to be emerging in some industries between Japan and certain other countries is in large part a reflection of the differences in business-support systems. So far, the Japanese system appears to have worked well. Will this continue to be the case? This is anybody's guess, but past success would indicate that the Japanese system certainly warrants consideration.

(September 1980)